Hidden Treasures

Hidden Treasures

Lesser-Known Freshwater Fish Species

Sam Loray

Grace Publishers

CONTENTS

INDEX 1

INTRODUCTION 3

1 | Chapter 1 16

2 | Chapter 2 35

3 | Chapter 3 52

4 | Chapter 4 72

5 | Chapter 5 93

6 | Chapter 6 111

7 | Chapter 7 130

8 | Chapter 8 149

INDEX

Introduction

1. Definition of "Hidden Treasures" in Freshwater
2. Importance of Lesser-Known Fish Species
3. Purpose of the Book

Chapter 1 Unveiling the Unknown
1.1 The Mystery Behind Lesser-Known Freshwater Fish
1.2 The Role of Lesser-Known Species in Ecosystems
1.3 Challenges in Studying and Identifying Hidden Treasures

Chapter 2 The Diverse World of Lesser-Known Freshwater Fish
2.1 Overview of Different Families and Genera
2.2 Unique Features and Adaptations
2.3 Geographical Distribution and Habitats

Chapter 3 The Ecological Significance
3.1 Lesser-Known Fish in Food Chains
3.2 Niche Specialization and Interactions
3.3 Conservation Concerns and Threats

Chapter 4 Fascinating Behaviors
4.1 Breeding Strategies and Reproductive Patterns
4.2 Feeding Habits and Foraging Techniques
4.3 Social Structures and Communication

Chapter 5 The Aquarium Enthusiast's Guide
5.1 Lesser-Known Fish Suitable for Home Aquariums
5.2 Tank Setup and Environmental Requirements
5.3 Tips for Breeding and Caring for Hidden Treasures

Chapter 6 Conservation Efforts
6.1 Endangered Lesser-Known Freshwater Fish
6.2 Success Stories in Conservation
6.3 How Individuals Can Contribute to Conservation

Chapter 7 Citizen Science and Research Opportunities
7.1 Involving the Public in Studying Lesser-Known Species
7.2 Collaborative Efforts with Scientists and Researchers
7.3 The Role of Technology in Discovering and Documenting Hidden Treasures

Chapter 8 Uncovering the Stories
8.1 Interviews with Biologists and Conservationists
8.2 Anecdotes and Stories from Fishermen and Local Communities
8.3 Historical Accounts and Legends Surrounding Lesser-Known Fish

INTRODUCTION

In the huge embroidery of freshwater biological systems, overflowing with life and variety, there exists a large number of animal categories that frequently get away from the spotlight. These are the secret fortunes, the less popular freshwater fish that assume pivotal parts in the sensitive equilibrium of sea-going biological systems. As we explore the mind boggling waters of this investigation, we set out on an excursion to uncover the mysteries, environmental importance, and stories that encompass these less popular pearls.

The Baffling Appeal of Less popular Freshwater Fish

Freshwater environments are dynamic and mind boggling, containing waterways, lakes, lakes, and streams that wind through scenes, interfacing assorted territories. While some fish species relax in the greatness of acknowledgment, others stay in the shadows, discreetly adding to the multifaceted dance of life submerged. The charm of these less popular species lies in their secret, a secret that entices us to dig into the profundities of their reality and unwind the mysteries they hold.

In this investigation, we rethink the expression "stowed away fortunes" to envelop not just the actual covering of these fish in the oceanic domain yet in addition the lack of clarity that encompasses their jobs in the environment. Past the magnetic megafauna that catch our consideration, there exists a universe of more modest, less obvious species that structure the foundation of freshwater biological systems. These are the uncelebrated yet truly great individuals, the unpretentious engineers of the amphibian scenes we frequently underestimate.

The Environmental Orchestra: Less popular Fish as Vital participants

As we peer underneath the surface, we find that these less popular fish species are not simple foundation players but rather key parts in the natural orchestra of freshwater conditions. Their jobs stretch out past the limits of their species; they are environment engineers, keeping up with the fragile equilibrium that supports life in and around water bodies.

Each less popular species adds to the unpredictable trap of connections inside its environment. From supplement cycling to controlling populace elements of prey species, these fish assume parts that are both nuanced and fundamental. Understanding

| 3 |

their natural importance isn't just a logical undertaking yet an excursion into the core of practical biological systems, where each specie, regardless of how little or unnoticeable, plays an indispensable part to play.

The Difficulties of Contemplating and Recognizing Stowed away Fortunes

In spite of their significance, the investigation of less popular freshwater fish presents a one of a kind arrangement of difficulties. Their subtle nature frequently makes them hard to notice and concentrate on in their regular territories. Ordered challenges further entangle endeavors to distinguish and arrange these species precisely. Thus, these fish stay stowed away from the public eye as well as from established researchers, obstructing how we might interpret their environment and conduct.

In this book, we defy these difficulties head-on, investigating the philosophies and advances that specialists utilize to reveal the mysteries of these secret fortunes. From state of the art hereditary strategies to resident science drives, the devices available to us are all around as different as the fish we look to comprehend. Through these endeavors, we desire to reveal insight into the less popular, making ready for a more extensive comprehension of freshwater biological systems.

The Reason for "Buried Fortunes: Less popular Freshwater Fish Species"

The reason for this book is complex. It, first and foremost, expects to bring these less popular fish species into the spotlight, offering a thorough investigation of their science, conduct, and environmental jobs. Furthermore, it looks to cultivate a more profound appreciation for the interconnectedness of all species inside freshwater biological systems. By understanding the meaning of these secret fortunes, we can more readily value the significance of preservation endeavors to save their living spaces.

Besides, "Covered up Fortunes" fills in as an aide for lovers, teachers, and preservationists the same. For aquarium lovers, we give bits of knowledge into less popular species reasonable for home aquariums, joined by down to earth tips for their consideration and reproducing. Teachers will track down an abundance of data to rouse interest in understudies about the frequently ignored miracles of freshwater environments. Finally, protectionists will find a source of inspiration, empowering them to advocate for the safeguarding of these secret fortunes and the living spaces they call home.

As we set out on this excursion into the profundities of freshwater environments, let us strip back the layers of secret encompassing these less popular fish species. Together, let us uncover the secret fortunes that hold the way in to the versatility and essentialness of our freshwater surroundings.

1. **Definition of "Hidden Treasures" in Freshwater**

    Freshwater environments, with their tangled waterways, peaceful lakes, and jabbering streams, are supplies of life abounding with a surprising variety of species. In this immense and multifaceted embroidered artwork of amphibian conditions, certain occupants remain clouded, eclipsed by their more alluring partners.

These subtle occupants, the unrecognized yet truly great individuals of freshwater environments, are the "covered up treasures" ready to be found and perceived. In disentangling the meaning of these secret fortunes, we explore through the intricacies of haziness, environmental importance, and the one of a kind difficulties that accompany concentrating on these less popular freshwater fish species.

Haziness Past the Surface

The expression "stowed away fortunes" with regards to freshwater biological systems stretches out past the actual camouflage of these species inside the water. It envelops the lack of clarity that covers them in the domain of public mindfulness and logical comprehension. While some fish species become notorious images, enhancing banners and aquariums, others unobtrusively explore the waters, to a great extent inconspicuous. These less prominent species, in any case, assume basic parts in keeping up with the wellbeing and equilibrium of their biological systems.

The lack of definition of these secret fortunes is a result of different elements. Actual attributes like size, shading, and environment inclinations add to their subtlety. Besides, ordered difficulties, where a few animal varieties intently look like others, worsen precisely recognizing and concentrating on them. Accordingly, large numbers of these fish stay in the shadowy domains of logical vagueness, avoiding the examination of the two specialists and the overall population.

Past Charming Megafauna: The Natural Worth of Less popular Species

To really get a handle on the embodiment of stowed away fortunes in freshwater biological systems, it is crucial for move past the charm of magnetic megafauna — the notable and outwardly striking species that catch our consideration. Less popular freshwater fish, however deficient with regards to the flashiness of their more renowned partners, have characteristic worth that reaches out a long ways past their actual appearances.

These secret fortunes are the modelers of balance inside freshwater environments. Their jobs might be unobtrusive, their commitments frequently disregarded, yet they are fundamental strings in the many-sided woven artwork of life. From keeping up with the fragile harmony between prey and hunter populaces to impacting supplement cycling inside environments, these unrecognized yet truly great individuals assume parts that are major to the prosperity of their living spaces.

Environment Architects in Camouflage

Consider the benthic tenants, the little species that filter through dregs looking for food. Their apparently everyday exercises have significant ramifications for the strength of freshwater conditions.

By working up residue, they add to supplement cycling, affecting the accessibility of fundamental components for different living beings in the biological system. These secret specialists shape the actual underpinning of the natural surroundings they possess.

Moreover, numerous less popular species act as key parts in food networks, possessing pivotal places that manage the wealth of different life forms. Their cooperations with both biotic and abiotic components make a sensitive dance, where every development has repercussions all through the biological system. Understanding these jobs isn't just a logical pursuit yet a door to valuing the interconnectedness of life in freshwater environments.

Challenges in Concentrating on Secret Fortunes

The way to understanding and characterizing stowed away fortunes in freshwater is loaded down with difficulties. The very qualities that make these fish unnoticeable likewise render them slippery subjects for logical review. Noticing their ways of behaving, concentrating on their life cycles, and interpreting their natural jobs require fastidious exertion and imaginative methodologies.

One of the essential difficulties lies in scientific classification. The grouping and recognizable proof of species are many-sided assignments, and the similitudes between specific less popular species and their all the more notable family members can jumble even the most prepared taxonomists. Recognizing firmly related species turns into a riddle, with hereditary examinations turning into a fundamental device in disentangling these ordered secrets.

The slippery idea of stowed away fortunes likewise presents difficulties for scientists expecting to notice these fish in their regular territories. Numerous species occupy remote or hard to-arrive at areas, and their ways of behaving might be adjusted in bondage, making it vital for concentrate on them in their regular habitats. This requires the utilization of cutting edge innovations like submerged cameras, remotely worked vehicles (ROVs), and even robots to catch slippery minutes in the existences of these less popular fish.

The Crossing point of Science and Preservation

Characterizing stowed away fortunes in freshwater stretches out past the domains of scholastic request; it is unpredictably connected with the basic of preservation. As we endeavor to comprehend these species, we all the while perceive the earnestness of safeguarding their environments. Freshwater biological systems overall face uncommon dangers — from natural surroundings annihilation and contamination to environmental change. Numerous less popular species, previously living on the edges of mindfulness, are doubly helpless against these anthropogenic tensions.

Preservation endeavors focusing on secret fortunes are many times complex. By and large, the absence of extensive information about these species represents a critical obstacle. Be that as it may, this information hole shouldn't block protection yet rather act as a source of inspiration. The prudent rule becomes central: even without complete comprehension, we should act to safeguard these species and their natural surroundings.

From Aquarists to Protectionists: Overcoming any barrier

In the domain of human collaboration with stowed away fortunes, aquarium fans assume a crucial part. For the people who track down euphoria in making oceanic biological systems inside the limits of a glass tank, the investigation of less popular species opens new roads. Aquariums give a window into the submerged world, permitting fans to see the value in the excellence and complexities of these frequently ignored fish.

The dependable consideration of less popular species in home aquariums can likewise add to protection endeavors. By developing an appreciation for the variety and uniqueness of these fish, aquarium lovers become envoys for the preservation cause. Besides, effective rearing and cultivation programs inside the aquarium local area can act as protection populaces for imperiled or compromised species, giving a security net against the hazards they face in nature.

Instructive Open doors: Supporting an Association with Stowed away Fortunes

Past the limits of home aquariums, the investigation of stowed away fortunes offers rich instructive open doors. In homerooms, nature focuses, and aquariums, teachers can utilize the tales of these less popular species to motivate interest and ecological stewardship in understudies. By presenting the intriguing universe of freshwater biological systems from the perspective of stowed away fortunes, teachers can ingrain a feeling of obligation for the safeguarding of these conditions.

Intelligent encounters, for example, field excursions and resident science drives, can carry understudies nearer to the secret fortunes in their nearby water bodies. The distinguishing proof of oceanic organic entities, figuring out their natural jobs, and taking part in preservation activities can change understudies into educated advocates for the assurance regarding freshwater biological systems.

Resident Science: A Cooperative Way to deal with Revelation

The journey to characterize and comprehend stowed away fortunes isn't bound to the domains of the scholarly world. Resident researchers, people energetic about the regular world, assume an essential part in extending our insight into less popular freshwater fish.

Their perceptions, frequently crossing different geographic areas, add to a more extensive comprehension of species circulation, conduct, and natural surroundings inclinations.

The combination of resident science into the investigation of stowed away fortunes encourages a feeling of local area commitment and shared liability regarding the prosperity of freshwater environments. Projects that include volunteers in information assortment, whether through water quality observing, fish counts, or natural surroundings appraisals, enhance the extent of logical request. The coordinated effort among researchers and resident researchers rises above customary limits, bringing about a more all encompassing and comprehensive way to deal with the investigation of less popular species.

Mechanical Advances: Enlightening the Profundities

As we explore the difficulties of concentrating on secret fortunes, innovation arises as a guide enlightening the profundities of freshwater biological systems. Progresses in submerged imaging, DNA examination, and telemetry give specialists uncommon apparatuses to disentangle the secrets of these less popular fish species.

Submerged cameras and ROVs offer windows into the secret existences of freshwater fish, catching ways of behaving that were once tricky. These mechanical wonders empower researchers to notice species in their normal natural surroundings without upsetting the fragile equilibrium of their biological systems. In addition, the utilization of ecological DNA (eDNA) permits scientists to identify the presence of species in water tests, altering the observing of slippery and jeopardized freshwater fish.

Social Importance: Stories, Legends, and Customs

Secret fortunes in freshwater biological systems are logical peculiarities as well as social substances, implanted in the narratives, legends, and customs of networks living in closeness to these water bodies. Native information frequently holds important experiences into the way of behaving, dissemination, and natural jobs of less popular fish species.

By integrating neighborhood stories and customary biological information into logical examination, a more all encompassing comprehension of stowed away fortunes arises. The convergence of logical request and social insight enhances our investigation, offering a nuanced viewpoint that rises above customary scholarly limits.

The Source of inspiration: Appreciation, Protection, and Proceeded with Investigation

As we finish up this investigation into the meaning of stowed away fortunes in freshwater biological systems, a reverberating source of inspiration reverberations through the profundities.

The enthusiasm for these less popular fish species isn't just a scholastic pursuit; it is an affirmation of the interconnectedness of life in freshwater conditions. It is an acknowledgment that each specie, regardless of how unnoticeable, assumes an essential part in the multifaceted snare of connections that supports these environments.

Preservation turns into an ethical objective, driven by the criticalness of safeguarding the charming megafauna as well as the secret fortunes that structure the foundation of freshwater natural surroundings. A guarantee to natural surroundings safeguarding, economical practices, and support for the security of imperiled species is fundamental to guarantee the strength of these biological systems for people in the future.

Our excursion into the meaning of stowed away fortunes doesn't close here however stretches out into the strange waters of proceeded with investigation. Innovative headways, cooperative endeavors, and the interest of people will impel us into new domains of revelation. The secret fortunes of freshwater biological systems, when clouded by the profundities, allure us to reveal their secrets, appreciate their importance, and champion their goal in the continuous story of natural preservation.

2. **Importance of Lesser-Known Fish Species**

In the unpredictable embroidery of freshwater biological systems, where life entwines in a sensitive dance, the significance of less popular fish species arises as a principal string. While the spotlight frequently falls upon magnetic megafauna, the subtle inhabitants of these amphibian domains assume basic parts that shape the wellbeing and essentialness of their surroundings. To unwind the meaning of these less popular species is to disentangle the actual texture of freshwater environments, where each occupant, regardless of how unobtrusive, adds to the complex equilibrium of life.

Biodiversity and Environment Versatility

At the core of the significance of less popular fish species lies the idea of biodiversity — the assortment of life structures inside an environment. Biodiversity isn't just a proportion of animal categories wealth yet an impression of the intricacy and versatility of biological systems. Less popular fish, with their variety in structure, capability, and natural specialties, add to the general biodiversity of freshwater environments.

Every species, regardless of its size or perceivability, possesses a one of a kind specialty inside the biological system. From base dwelling species that filter through silt to channel feeders that add to supplement cycling, the practical variety of these less popular fish is a demonstration of the flexibility and adaptability of freshwater biological systems. Biodiversity improves the versatility of biological systems, improving them prepared to endure natural changes, illnesses, and different unsettling influences.

Supplement Cycling and Water Quality

Secret underneath the water's surface, less popular fish species assume critical parts in supplement cycling — a crucial biological interaction that impacts the accessibility of fundamental components inside freshwater environments. A significant number of these species, through their taking care of propensities and ways of behaving, add to the breakdown of natural matter and the reusing of supplements.

Base dwelling species, like catfish and loaches, upset silt as they rummage for food, advancing the disintegration of natural material. This interaction discharges supplements once more into the water, making a powerful cycle that supports the efficiency of the biological system. The presence and exercises of these less popular fish straightforwardly influence water quality, affecting elements like supplement levels, turbidity, and in general biological system wellbeing.

Guideline of Prey Populaces
In the many-sided snare of freshwater food networks, less popular fish frequently assume the part of both hunter and prey. Their cooperations with different creatures direct populace elements, forestalling the uncontrolled multiplication of specific species. By originating before on more modest organic entities, these fish assist with keeping an equilibrium that forestalls the overconsumption of assets and the resulting destabilization of the environment.

The guideline of prey populaces by less popular fish isn't just about keeping up with natural equilibrium yet additionally about supporting the variety of life. Certain species might work in consuming explicit sorts of prey, forestalling the strength of any one animal groups and considering the concurrence of a large number of life forms inside the environment.

Pointer Species and Ecological Wellbeing
The strength of freshwater biological systems is unpredictably connected to the prosperity of their occupants. Less popular fish species, frequently delicate to changes in their current circumstance, can act as important signs of environment wellbeing. Their presence, overflow, and conduct can give bits of knowledge into the general state of the water body, flagging likely natural stressors or contamination.

In the domain of preservation and natural checking, the perception of less popular fish turns into a device for evaluating the effect of human exercises on freshwater environments. Changes in water quality, natural surroundings corruption, or the presentation of obtrusive species can appear in the ways of behaving and populaces of these pointer species, offering early admonitions that brief further examination and mediation.

Financial and Sporting Worth
Past their natural commitments, less popular fish species hold monetary and sporting worth. In numerous areas, these fish structure the premise of neighborhood fisheries, supporting the livelihoods of networks subject to freshwater assets. While specific species may not arrive at the business meaning of notable fish like salmon or trout, they regardless add to the dietary requirements and monetary food of nearby populaces.

Additionally, less popular fish species frequently give open doors to sporting fishermen. Plotting for less popular species, in some cases alluded to as "harsh fish," has its own allure, drawing in aficionados who look for the excitement of getting exceptional and more uncommon fish. This sporting perspective adds to the social meaning of these species, encouraging an association among individuals and the frequently neglected occupants of freshwater environments.

Strength to Ecological Changes

The flexibility and strength of less popular fish species are key credits that add to the general versatility of freshwater environments. While certain species might be trained professionals, finely tuned to explicit territories and conditions, others show striking versatility, flourishing in different conditions. This flexibility permits them to endure vacillations in temperature, water stream, and other natural factors.

Even with environmental change, where freshwater biological systems are encountering adjusted precipitation designs, climbing temperatures, and changes in living space accessibility, the strength of these less popular species becomes fundamental. They act as marks of the capacity of freshwater biological systems to adapt to and recuperate from ecological changes, adding to how we might interpret the drawn out manageability of these imperative territories.

Saving Hereditary Variety

The hereditary variety inside populaces of less popular fish species is a supply of likely variations and developmental versatility. Safeguarding the hereditary variety of these species is urgent for their capacity to answer ecological changes, including those actuated by human exercises. Hereditary variety improves the developmental capability of populaces, permitting them to adjust to moving circumstances over the long run.

Saving the hereditary variety of less popular fish isn't just an interest in that frame of mind of individual species yet in addition a more extensive methodology for shielding the biodiversity and biological trustworthiness of freshwater environments. It is an acknowledgment that the safeguarding of species remains closely connected with the protection of the interesting hereditary legacy they convey.

Instructive Open doors and Logical Revelation

The investigation of less popular fish species gives unrivaled instructive open doors and roads for logical revelation. From the littlest feeders to the biggest lakes, these fish occupy different environments that offer an abundance of opportunities for natural examination. Concentrating on their ways of behaving, conceptive methodologies, and cooperations with different species extends how we might interpret the complexities of freshwater biological systems.

For understudies and scientists the same, less popular fish species present a material for investigation and examination. Their frequently undocumented lives welcome logical request, empowering the improvement of new strategies and advances for concentrating on these subtle animals. Instructive drives revolved around these species cultivate a feeling of miracle and interest, sustaining the up and coming age of researchers and natural stewards.

The Interconnected Web: A Call to Appreciate and Save

Basically, the significance of less popular fish species is woven into the actual texture of freshwater biological systems. These frequently disregarded occupants add to the strength, biodiversity, and generally speaking soundness of amphibian conditions. As we explore the intricate waters of preservation and feasible administration, it becomes clear that appreciating and understanding these less popular species isn't a choice however a need.

Preservation endeavors should stretch out past the magnetic megafauna to envelop the sum of freshwater biological systems, perceiving the interconnectedness, everything being equal, apparent and stowed away. Safeguarding the territories that help these less popular fish is a pledge to the protection of the sensitive equilibrium that supports life in waterways, lakes, and streams around the world.

The call to appreciate and monitor less popular fish species is a call to perceive the inborn worth of each and every life form inside freshwater environments. It is an acknowledgment that the wellbeing of these environments is an impression of our aggregate liability to defend the normal world. In the flows of ecological stewardship, understanding and esteeming the significance of these less popular fortunes is a navigational reference point directing us toward a future where the lavishness of freshwater life perseveres.

3. **Purpose of the Book**

Chasing information and understanding, the investigation of stowed away fortunes in freshwater biological systems becomes the overwhelming focus in the book named **"Stowed away Fortunes:** Less popular Freshwater Fish Species." This scholarly undertaking isn't only a gathering of statistical data points; it is an excursion into the profundities of sea-going domains, an investigation of the secrets, environmental importance, and social stories that encompass the less popular fish species possessing our waterways, lakes, and streams. The reason for this book is multi-layered, intending to illuminate, motivate, and advocate for the preservation of these frequently disregarded pearls of the oceanic world.

1. **Bringing issues to light: Uncovering Stowed away Fortunes**

    At the core of the book's motivation is the mission to bring issues to light about the presence and significance of less popular freshwater fish species. These uncelebrated yet truly great individuals of sea-going biological systems frequently stay in lack of clarity, eclipsed by their all the more outwardly striking partners. By devoting an exhaustive investigation to these less popular species, the book tries to focus on their remarkable qualities, ways of behaving, and environmental jobs.

Through distinctive depictions, connecting with accounts, and dazzling symbolism, the book endeavors to bring perusers into the submerged universes where these secret fortunes flourish. By winding around together logical experiences, stories, and social points of view, the point is to make a story that rises above the limits of conventional logical talk, making the topic open and connecting with for a different crowd.

2. **Cultivating Appreciation: Finding the Excellence in the Inconspicuous**

Appreciation is a foundation of protection. To think often about the conservation of an animal varieties or territory, one must initially see the value in its magnificence, uniqueness, and significance. The book tries to cultivate a profound appreciation for the less popular fish species that add to the rich embroidery of freshwater biological systems. It welcomes perusers to see past the surface and perceive the natural worth of these frequently disregarded amphibian occupants.

Through distinctive depictions of the different structures, ways of behaving, and environments of less popular fish, the book illustrates the excellence that exists underneath the water's surface. It challenges biases about what is a "charming" species and welcomes perusers to track down wonder in the unpretentious complexities of the sea-going world. By ingraining a feeling of wonder and deference, the book intends to develop an enduring association among perusers and the secret fortunes of freshwater environments.

3. **Instruction and Effort: Engaging Fans and Backers**

Instruction is an incredible asset for preservation. The book fills in as an instructive asset, giving an abundance of data about less popular fish species, their biological jobs, and the difficulties they face.

Focusing on a different crowd, from understudies and teachers to aquarium lovers and resident researchers, the book enables people to become educated advocates for the protection regarding freshwater environments.

For instructors, the book offers an educational program rich investigation of freshwater nature, presenting less popular fish species as central focuses for examples on biodiversity, biological relationship, and ecological stewardship. Through contextual investigations, tales, and meetings with specialists, the book gives a dynamic and drawing in instructive experience that reaches out past the bounds of conventional study hall learning.

Aquarium lovers, attracted to the charm of submerged universes, track down in the book a manual for integrating less popular species into their home aquariums capably. Reasonable exhortation on tank arrangement, care, and rearing is supplemented by a more profound comprehension of the natural jobs these fish play, upgrading the specialist experience with a feeling of ecological obligation.

Resident researchers, enthusiastic about adding to logical information, find in the book a source of inspiration. By participating in projects connected with the observing and protection of less popular fish species, people can become dynamic members in the logical cycle. The book features the job of resident science in growing comprehension we might interpret these secret fortunes and stresses the significance of cooperative endeavors in the mission for information.

4. **Protection Basic: Asking Activity for the Secret Fortunes**
The book is in excess of a festival of the excellence and variety of less popular fish species; it is a source of inspiration for their protection. As freshwater biological systems overall face uncommon dangers, from natural surroundings annihilation to contamination and environmental change, the book highlights the weakness of these frequently disregarded species. It verbalizes the pressing requirement for proactive preservation measures to save their natural surroundings and guarantee the endurance of these secret fortunes.

Protection isn't exclusively the obligation of researchers and policymakers; an aggregate undertaking requires the cooperation of people, networks, and associations. The book gives experiences into the particular preservation challenges looked by less popular fish species, offering an indisputable case for why these species merit consideration and insurance. By winding around together logical proof with genuine instances of effective preservation drives, the book motivates trust and exhibits that positive change is conceivable.

Through interviews with preservationists, specialists, and local area pioneers, the book exhibits the variety of ways to deal with protection.

It features the job of nearby networks in defending their freshwater assets and stresses the significance of cooperative drives that overcome any barrier between logical information and grassroots activity. In doing as such, the book fills in as an aide for people and associations anxious to add to the protection of freshwater environments and their secret fortunes.

5. **Moral Contemplations: Supporting a Capable Relationship with Nature**
Morals and capable commitment with the regular world are necessary to the book's motivation. As perusers dig into the miracles of less popular fish species, the book urges an intelligent way to deal with mankind's relationship with the climate. It prompts examination about the moral ramifications of our activities and the results of dismissing the conservation of biodiversity in freshwater environments.

The book dives into the moral contemplations of the aquarium exchange, the effect of living space obliteration on freshwater territories, and the moral obligations of analysts and devotees the same. It advocates for a moral system that focuses on the prosperity of biological systems and their occupants, elevating rehearses that add to the maintainability and strength of freshwater conditions.

6. **Developing Interest and Miracle: Moving the Up and coming Age of Travelers**

In the soul of logical disclosure and investigation, the book tries to light interest and miracle. By introducing the secret fortunes of freshwater environments as subjects of interest and secret, the book allures perusers, youthful and old, to set out on their own excursions of investigation. From the perspective of less popular fish species, the book shows that there is something else to learn, find, and value in the regular world.

For youthful perusers, the book fills in as a prologue to the marvels of freshwater biological systems, igniting an early interest in the inherent sciences and ecological preservation. By winding around together logical realities with enamoring stories, the book makes a story that is both instructive and engaging, cultivating an adoration for learning and an appreciation for the intricacies of the normal world.

Chapter 1

Unveiling the Unknown

In the tremendous spreads of freshwater environments, underneath the intelligent surfaces of lakes, wandering streams, and quiet lakes, lies a domain of secret and miracle. Inconspicuous, frequently inconspicuous, there exists a variety of less popular fish species, their lives weaved with the many-sided woven artwork of oceanic scenes. In this excursion of disclosure, we dig into the obscure, looking to reveal the secrets that cover these secret fortunes. From the confounding profundities of their ways of behaving to the ordered riddles that challenge specialists, we leave on an investigation that rises above the surface, welcoming perusers to go with us into the profundities of the unexplored world.

The Secret World Underneath the Surface
The Secret Behind Less popular Freshwater Fish

The investigation of the obscure starts with an assessment of the actual pith of less popular freshwater fish. What renders them stowed away? What secrets exist in the profundities of their ways of behaving, territories, and transformations? This section digs into the complexities of these species, revealing the elements that add to their puzzling nature.

From their genuine appearances to their frequently obscure ways of behaving, we disclose the layers that disguise these sea-going puzzles.

The Job of Less popular Species in Biological systems

Past their secret, the main section explores the basic jobs less popular species play inside freshwater environments. How do these secret fortunes add to the natural equilibrium? Through a point by point investigation of their associations with different life forms, their effect on supplement cycling, and their situations in unpredictable food networks, we shed light on the fundamental capabilities these species satisfy. This part expects to uncover the interconnectedness of the amphibian world, underscoring the meaning of these less popular species in supporting the sensitive harmony of freshwater conditions.

Challenges in Considering and Recognizing Stowed away Fortunes

As we leave on the excursion to divulge the obscure, the section closes by tending to the difficulties analysts face in considering and recognizing less popular freshwater fish. Ordered complexities, the tricky idea of these species, and the impediments of customary exploration techniques present obstacles to grasping their secrets.

This segment makes way for resulting sections, indicating the inventive techniques and advancements expected to disentangle the mysteries of these secret fortunes.

The Different Universe of Less popular Freshwater Fish
Outline of Various Families and Genera

In the subsequent part, our investigation broadens to envelop the assorted exhibit of less popular freshwater fish. From the profundities of streams to the shallows of lakes, these species range different families and genera, each contributing an interesting string to the embroidery of sea-going life. The section fills in as a prologue to the captivating variety that anticipates, featuring the particular elements that characterize these less popular pearls.

Extraordinary Elements and Transformations

Diving further, we divulge the one of a kind elements and transformations that portray less popular fish species. From particular physical designs to social variations sharpened by development, this segment uncovers the multifaceted systems that permit these species to flourish in their separate environments. It is an excursion into the secret universe of natural wonders, exhibiting the flexibility and versatility implanted in the hereditary codes of less popular fish.

Topographical Conveyance and Environments

The part finishes up by investigating the topographical conveyance of less popular species and the assorted territories they call home. From the sweeping Amazon rainforest to the quiet pools of Africa, the secret fortunes are conveyed across the globe, adjusting to a large number of conditions. Understanding the geology and living spaces of these species gives fundamental setting to valuing their importance in the more extensive setting of worldwide freshwater biological systems.

The Biological Meaning of Less popular Freshwater Fish

Less popular Fish in Pecking orders

As we unwind the biological meaning of less popular freshwater fish, we direct our concentration toward their parts in pecking orders. This part looks at the complexities of hunter prey connections, the effect of these species on more modest organic entities, and the far reaching influences they make inside amphibian environments. By looking into the intricacies of food networks, we uncover the fundamental position these secret fortunes involve.

Specialty Specialization and Connections

Expanding upon the comprehension of pecking orders, this segment investigates the idea of specialty specialization among less popular fish species.

How do these species cut out their environmental specialties? What cooperations happen between various species going after restricted assets? The section analyzes the elements of specialty specialization and natural collaborations, enlightening the sensitive equilibrium kept up with by these frequently ignored occupants of freshwater biological systems.

Preservation Concerns and Dangers

Notwithstanding, the natural meaning of less popular freshwater fish accompanies a sobering reality — preservation concerns and dangers. This part reveals insight into the difficulties these species face, going from territory annihilation to contamination and environmental change. By disentangling the dangers presented to these secret fortunes, the section accentuates the criticalness of protection endeavors to guarantee the proceeded with presence of these confounding species.

Interesting Ways of behaving

Rearing Methodologies and Regenerative Examples

In the investigation of the obscure, the center movements to the captivating ways of behaving displayed by less popular freshwater fish. This part explores through the complexities of their rearing systems and conceptive examples. From novel romance ceremonies to unpredictable conceptive techniques, we uncover the assorted manners by which these species guarantee the continuation of their genealogies. The part gives a brief look into the secret universe of fish conceptive science, displaying the creativity implanted in their ways of behaving.

Taking care of Propensities and Scrounging Strategies

Past propagation, the part investigates the taking care of propensities and scrounging methods that less popular fish utilize to make due in their separate environments. Whether they are channel feeders, herbivores, or hunters with specific hunting strategies, every species adds to the general working of their environments. By disentangling the secrets of their taking care of ways of behaving, we gain knowledge into the biological jobs played by these frequently neglected sea-going occupants.

Social Designs and Correspondence

The investigation of captivating ways of behaving finishes in an assessment of the social designs and specialized strategies displayed by less popular freshwater fish. While certain species display singular ways of behaving, others structure complicated interpersonal organizations.

The section digs into the correspondence methodologies utilized by these species, whether through visual showcases, substance prompts, or acoustic signs.

By unwinding the intricacies of their public activities, we uncover one more layer of the obscure, testing assumptions about the social elements of less popular fish.

The Aquarium Fan's Aide
Less popular Fish Appropriate for Home Aquariums

For aquarium fans looking to bring the marvels of freshwater environments into their homes, the book gives a manual for less popular fish reasonable for home aquariums. This segment presents an organized choice of animal categories, each joined by experiences into their consideration necessities, similarity with different species, and the remarkable elements that make them enamoring increases to aquariums. It is a scaffold between the secret profundities of regular territories and the organized biological systems of aquariums, permitting devotees to appreciate and moderate less popular species inside the bounds of their homes.

Tank Arrangement and Ecological Necessities

Common sense is central for aquarium lovers, and this segment offers direction on making appropriate tank arrangements for less popular fish. From water boundaries to substrate decisions, the section gives an extensive outline of the ecological prerequisites that imitate the regular territories of these species. By diving into the complexities of tank arrangement, the book intends to engage devotees to give ideal circumstances to the prosperity of their oceanic sidekicks.

Preservation Contemplations in Aquarium Keeping

The section finishes up with a conversation on preservation contemplations in aquarium keeping. Capable and moral practices are fundamental for guaranteeing that the fame of less popular fish in the aquarium exchange doesn't add to their decrease in nature. By advancing attention to protection issues and pushing for feasible aquarium rehearses, the book urges aquarium lovers to become advocates for the safeguarding of these secret fortunes.

Resident Science and Cooperative Investigation
The Job of Resident Science in Divulging the Unexplored world

In the soul of joint effort and shared investigation, the book digs into the job of resident science in divulging the unexplored world. This part features the important commitments of resident researchers in information assortment, checking, and research connected with less popular freshwater fish. By enhancing the effect of individual perceptions and cultivating a feeling of local area commitment, resident science arises as an integral asset in the journey to extend how we might interpret these cryptic species.

Cooperative Ventures and Drives

Expanding upon the idea of resident science, this part investigates cooperative tasks and drives that unite researchers, scientists, and devotees in a common work to disclose the secrets of freshwater biological systems. From people group driven checking projects to cooperative examination attempts, the section grandstands instances of effective drives that overcome any issues among experts and energetic people. It is a source of inspiration for cooperative investigation and a demonstration of the capability of aggregate endeavors in progressing logical information.

Mechanical Advances and Development
Submerged Cameras, ROVs, and Robots: Enlightening the Profundities

As we venture further into the obscure, innovation arises as a directing light, enlightening the profundities of freshwater biological systems. This part investigates the mechanical advances that have upset the investigation of less popular fish species. Submerged cameras, remotely worked vehicles (ROVs), and drones offer remarkable admittance to the secret existences of these amphibian occupants. By exhibiting the abilities of these advancements, the part divulges the imaginative instruments that specialists use to defeat the difficulties of concentrating on subtle and frequently unavailable species.

Natural DNA (eDNA) and Hereditary Investigations

The investigation of mechanical advances reaches out to the domain of atomic biology. Natural DNA (eDNA) and hereditary examinations have changed our capacity to recognize and concentrate on less popular fish species without direct perception. By dissecting hints of DNA shed into the climate, analysts can uncover the presence of species, disentangle their hereditary variety, and investigate their transformative chronicles. This part dives into the sub-atomic apparatuses that add to the thorough comprehension of stowed away fortunes in freshwater environments.

Social Importance and Native Information

Stories, Legends, and Customs: The Social Setting of Less popular Fish

The investigation of the obscure takes on a social aspect as the book explores the narratives, legends, and customs related with less popular fish species. Native information, went down through ages, frequently holds important bits of knowledge into the ways of behaving, natural jobs, and social meaning of these oceanic occupants. By winding around together logical request and social insight, this section offers a nuanced viewpoint that improves our investigation of stowed away fortunes.

Social Protection Practices

Understanding the social meaning of less popular fish species opens an entryway to investigating social protection rehearses. This segment dives into instances of how networks incorporate customary information and practices into preservation endeavors. By perceiving the interconnectedness of social and biological qualities, the book underlines the significance of cooperative methodologies that regard and coordinate native points of view in the protection of freshwater environments.

Protection Systems and Difficulties

Preservation Systems for Less popular Freshwater Fish

The source of inspiration repeats boisterously in this part, as the book frames preservation techniques for less popular freshwater fish. From environment protection to reasonable administration rehearses, the segment gives a guide to shielding the fate of these mysterious species. It digs into the intricacies of protection arranging, underlining the requirement for interdisciplinary methodologies that think about natural, social, and social variables.

Difficulties and Arrangements

Be that as it may, the way to protection isn't without challenges. This segment investigates the obstacles and obstructions looked in the preservation of less popular fish species. From subsidizing requirements to the intricacies of worldwide cooperation, the part tends to the barriers that hinder viable protection endeavors. By recognizing the difficulties, the book looks to rouse versatility and development despite difficulty.

The Strange Eventual fate of Investigation

Progressions, Disclosures, and the Continuous Investigation

In the last section, the book turns its look toward the fate of investigation. What progressions and disclosures anticipate as we keep on divulging the unexplored world? This segment gives a brief look into continuous exploration, state of the art innovations, and the potential for new disclosures about less popular freshwater fish species. It is a demonstration of the persevering through soul of investigation and the vast conceivable outcomes that lie ahead in our mission to figure out the secret fortunes of oceanic biological systems.

Training, Backing, and Proceeded with Interest

The section closes by underlining the continuous jobs of training and support in sustaining a feeling of obligation for the protection of freshwater environments. As the excursion into the obscure proceeds, the book approaches people, networks, and associations to encourage a culture of interest, protection, and appreciation for the secrets that lie underneath the water's surface.

It is a challenge to set out on an excursion of long lasting learning and investigation, guaranteeing that the mission to disclose the obscure remaining parts a persevering and extraordinary pursuit.

1.1 The Mystery Behind Lesser-Known Freshwater Fish

In the peaceful scenes of freshwater biological systems, underneath the gleaming impressions of daylight, a secret world unfurls — one possessed by less popular freshwater fish species. The charm of the obscure calls, covered in secret and interest. As we set out on the investigation of these puzzling oceanic occupants, the main part of our process disentangles the shroud that hide the secrets behind less popular freshwater fish.

The Honest Exteriors: What Renders Them Stowed away?

From the start, less popular freshwater fish frequently have honest appearances, without any trace of the dynamic tones and affected sizes that portray more natural species. Their nuance permits them to mix flawlessly into their living spaces, delivering them unnoticeable to the easygoing eyewitness. This unpretentious nature, notwithstanding, gives a false representation of the complex transformations and ways of behaving that characterize their reality.

These fish have advanced to explore the intricacies of their surroundings with artfulness, from smoothed out bodies that float through thick vegetation to obscure tinge that covers them against riverbeds and rough substrates. The secret falsehoods in their actual attributes as well as in the techniques they utilize to evade recognition, making them subtle and testing subjects for logical review.

Mysterious Ways of behaving: Exploring the Shadows

Past their honest outsides, the ways of behaving of less popular freshwater fish add layers to the secret. These species frequently show mysterious ways of behaving, deciding to stay in the shadows and stay stowed away from the two hunters and scientists the same. Their slippery nature represents a test to researchers trying to unwind the complexities of their lives.

Numerous less popular species are nighttime, branching out under the front of dimness to take care of and replicate. This way of behaving, combined with their inclination for separated environments, adds to the emanation of secret encompassing their regular routines. Concentrating on these fish requires persistence, inventive exploration strategies, and a sharp comprehension of their natural surroundings to catch looks at their ways of behaving that happen past the range of sunlight.

Variations to Sidestep Discovery: A Method for surviving

Endurance in the sea-going domain depends on the capacity to adjust and avoid recognition. Less popular freshwater fish have sharpened their transformative ability to explore their territories without drawing unnecessary consideration. A few animal types, for instance, display a dominance of disguise, reflecting the varieties and examples of their environmental factors to become indistinct from the oceanic greenery that wraps them.

Their variations go past the visual domain, reaching out to tactile components that permit them to distinguish unpretentious changes in their current circumstance. The parallel line framework, for example, empowers them to see vibrations and developments, offering an elevated mindfulness that guides in both hunter evasion and prey catch. These variations highlight the intricacy of their reality, divulging an existence where endurance depends on a sensitive harmony between covering and insight.

Ordered Riddles: The Test of ID

As we dive into the secrets of less popular freshwater fish, the ordered domain presents one more layer of intricacy. ID challenges endure, for certain species intently looking like one another or showing varieties in actual attributes in light of their geographic areas. The complexities of scientific classification add a layer of secret, inciting specialists to utilize progressed strategies, including sub-atomic examinations, to perceive the uniqueness of every species.

The obscured lines between firmly related species add to the difficulties of arrangement and figuring out the full extent of biodiversity inside freshwater environments. The secrets of scientific categorization reach out past the profundities of streams and lakes, winding around a story of interconnectedness that rises above customary limits.

The Unseen Domains: Environments and Locales Neglected

The living spaces that less popular freshwater fish call home contribute altogether to their slippery nature. A significant number of these species possess remote or hard to-arrive at areas, where the profundities of the obscure remain to a great extent neglected. From the cloudy waters of thickly vegetated marshes to the secret openings of underground caverns, these fish explore conditions that current difficulties to the two specialists and lovers.

The geographic dissemination of these species traverses the globe, enveloping districts that are still somewhat neglected regarding freshwater biodiversity. The unseen regions hold the commitment of new species anticipating ID and give a brief look into the endlessness of sea-going environments yet to be completely perceived.

1.2 The Role of Lesser-Known Species in Ecosystems

In the multifaceted embroidery of freshwater environments, where life entwines in a fragile dance, the job of less popular fish species arises as a principal string. While alluring megafauna frequently get everyone's attention, these unnoticeable occupants assume pivotal parts that shape the wellbeing and essentialness of their surroundings. To disentangle the meaning of these less popular species is to reveal the actual texture of freshwater biological systems, where each organic entity, regardless of how unobtrusive, adds to the mind boggling equilibrium of life.

Biodiversity as the Establishment

At the core of the significance of less popular fish species lies the idea of biodiversity — the assortment of life structures inside an environment. Biodiversity isn't simply a proportion of animal varieties extravagance however an impression of the intricacy and versatility of environments. Less popular fish, with their variety in structure, capability, and environmental specialties, add to the general biodiversity of freshwater natural surroundings.

Every species, regardless of its size or perceivability, possesses an interesting specialty inside the biological system. From base dwelling species that filter through dregs to channel feeders that add to supplement cycling, the practical variety of these less popular fish is a demonstration of the flexibility and adaptability of freshwater environments.

Biodiversity improves the flexibility of biological systems, improving them prepared to endure natural changes, illnesses, and different unsettling influences. The many-sided snare of life in freshwater biological systems depends on the presence and cooperations of these less popular species to keep a sound and adjusted climate.

Supplement Cycling: Supporting Life Underneath the Surface

Secret underneath the water's surface, less popular fish species assume significant parts in supplement cycling — a major environmental interaction that impacts the accessibility of fundamental components inside freshwater biological systems. A large number of these species, through their taking care of propensities and ways of behaving, add to the breakdown of natural matter and the reusing of supplements.

Base dwelling species, like catfish and loaches, upset dregs as they rummage for food, advancing the decay of natural material. This interaction discharges supplements like nitrogen and phosphorus back into the water, making a unique cycle that supports the efficiency of the environment.

The nonstop reusing of supplements by less popular fish isn't just fundamental for the strength of the biological system yet additionally upholds the development of essential makers, like green growth and sea-going plants.

Along these lines, these subtle species in a roundabout way add to the food web, giving energy and assets to a huge number of creatures inside the freshwater climate.

Guideline of Prey Populaces: Keeping up with Biological Equilibrium

In the unpredictable snare of freshwater food networks, less popular fish frequently assume the parts of both hunter and prey. Their associations with different organic entities manage populace elements, forestalling the unrestrained multiplication of specific species. By originating before on more modest organic entities, these fish assist with keeping an equilibrium that forestalls the overconsumption of assets and the resulting destabilization of the environment.

The guideline of prey populaces by less popular fish isn't just about keeping up with natural equilibrium yet in addition about supporting the variety of life. Certain species might have practical experience in consuming explicit kinds of prey, forestalling the predominance of any one animal types and considering the conjunction of a huge number of creatures inside the biological system.

This fragile dance of hunter and prey is fundamental for the dependability of freshwater environments. The presence and exercises of less popular fish add to the mind boggling movement that guarantees the endurance and concurrence of a different exhibit of animal categories.

Marker Species: Sentinels of Natural Wellbeing

The soundness of freshwater environments is unpredictably connected to the prosperity of their occupants. Less popular fish species, frequently delicate to changes in their current circumstance, can act as significant marks of environment wellbeing. Their presence, overflow, and conduct can give experiences into the general state of the water body, flagging possible ecological stressors or contamination.

In the domain of protection and ecological checking, the perception of less popular fish turns into a device for evaluating the effect of human exercises on freshwater biological systems. Changes in water quality, environment debasement, or the presentation of obtrusive species can appear in the ways of behaving and populaces of these marker species, offering early alerts that brief further examination and mediation.

The job of pointer species reaches out past a simple impression of natural wellbeing; it highlights the interconnectedness of biological systems. By focusing on the prosperity of less popular fish, researchers and progressives gain important bits of knowledge into the more extensive strength of the whole freshwater biological system.

Financial and Sporting Worth: Supporting People group

Past their biological commitments, less popular fish species hold monetary and sporting worth. In numerous districts, these fish structure the premise of neighborhood fisheries, supporting the vocations of networks reliant upon freshwater assets.

While specific species may not arrive at the business meaning of notable fish like salmon or trout, they in any case add to the dietary requirements and financial food of nearby populaces.

Also, less popular fish species frequently give open doors to sporting fishermen. Plotting for less popular species, at times alluded to as "unpleasant fish," has its own allure, drawing in aficionados who look for the adventure of getting novel and more uncommon fish. This sporting perspective adds to the social meaning of these species, encouraging an association among individuals and the frequently ignored occupants of freshwater biological systems.

The financial and sporting worth of less popular fish isn't just a demonstration of their significance for nearby networks yet additionally highlights the requirement for feasible administration rehearses. Adjusting human use of these assets with the protection of environmental respectability is urgent to guarantee the proceeded with accessibility and wellbeing of less popular fish populaces.

Flexibility to Natural Changes: Adjusting for Endurance

The versatility and flexibility of less popular fish species are key ascribes that add to the general wellbeing and security of freshwater environments. These fish have developed methodologies to adapt to a scope of natural circumstances, from fluctuating water levels to changes in temperature and water quality.

Their capacity to flourish in assorted environments, incorporating those with restricted assets or testing conditions, makes them important supporters of biological system working. Notwithstanding ecological changes, including those determined by environmental change, the versatility of less popular fish can impact the generally speaking versatile limit of freshwater biological systems.

Difficulties and Protection Contemplations

While the jobs of less popular fish species in biological systems are critical, their populaces face various difficulties. Natural surroundings obliteration, contamination, overfishing, and the presentation of intrusive species present dangers to their endurance. The very qualities that make them significant supporters of biological systems —, for example, their frequently particular transformations — can likewise make them powerless against changes in their current circumstance.

Preservation endeavors should address these difficulties through a comprehensive methodology that thinks about the complicated connections inside freshwater biological systems. Safeguarding the living spaces of less popular fish, carrying out feasible fishing rehearses, and alleviating the effects of contamination are vital parts of protection systems.

1.3 Challenges in Studying and Identifying Hidden Treasures

Setting out on the excursion to study and distinguish less popular freshwater fish species is much the same as exploring the pit — a domain covered in secret, intricacy, and various difficulties. As researchers dive into the profundities of oceanic environments to disentangle the insider facts of these secret fortunes, they defy deterrents that request imaginative methodologies, interdisciplinary joint effort, and a profound comprehension of the complexities that characterize the existences of these frequently disregarded occupants.

Ordered Complexities: The Riddle of Characterization

At the core of the difficulties in concentrating on less popular freshwater fish lies the perplexing riddle of scientific classification. The method involved with characterizing and recognizing species is many times more going on under the surface. While some fish might have unmistakable morphological highlights, others display varieties that jumble conventional arrangement techniques.

Obscure Species and Morphological Variety: Mysterious species, those that are morphologically comparative however hereditarily particular, represent a critical test. Customary morphological attributes utilized for recognizable proof may not enough catch the hereditary variety present inside apparently indistinguishable species. Thus, specialists should utilize progressed atomic procedures, for example, DNA barcoding and hereditary examinations, to recognize mysterious species and unwind the ordered complexities.

Geographic Variety: The geographic conveyance of less popular fish species adds one more layer of intricacy to ordered difficulties. Populaces of a solitary animal varieties might show varieties in tinge, size, or other morphological qualities in view of their geographic areas. Scientists should consider the ramifications of these varieties while endeavoring to characterize and recognize species, frequently requiring a nuanced comprehension of local contrasts.

Trickiness in Conduct: The Test of Perception

Concentrating on the way of behaving of less popular freshwater fish presents an interesting arrangement of difficulties due to their frequently subtle nature. Dissimilar to additional obvious species, these fish might show ways of behaving that happen in covered up, remote, or hard to-get to territories. This slipperiness requests intelligent fixes to precisely notice and archive their ways of behaving.

Nighttime Conduct: Numerous less popular species are nighttime, leading fundamental exercises like taking care of and proliferation under the front of haziness.

Noticing these ways of behaving in their regular environments represents a calculated test for scientists. Particular hardware, like submerged cameras with low-light capacities, and late evening plunging become fundamental instruments for catching the tricky exercises of these nighttime occupants.

Environment Inclinations: The natural surroundings picked by less popular fish, frequently separated or thickly vegetated regions, further confound the perception interaction. Analysts should explore testing territories, like lowered caves, marshy conditions, or profound riverbeds, to concentrate on these species in their regular settings. The actual requests of getting to these natural surroundings add an additional layer of intricacy to observational investigations.

Restricted Openness: The Secret Domains of Freshwater Environments

The very environments that encourage the uniqueness of less popular freshwater fish additionally add to the test of restricted availability. Not at all like marine conditions that are all the more promptly open for examination and investigation, freshwater biological systems can be hidden, remote, and testing to reach.

Underground Territories: Some less popular fish species possess underground conditions, like caverns and underground streams. Getting to these secret domains requires particular cavern jumping abilities, modern gear, and a careful comprehension of the difficulties presented by the underground scene.

Thick Vegetation and Far off Areas: Different species find shelter in thickly vegetated regions or distant areas that are not effectively reachable. Analysts might have to utilize creative examining procedures, like remotely worked vehicles (ROVs) or submerged drones, to explore through thick vegetation or arrive at distant territories.

Examining Inclination: The Concealed Results

The intrinsic difficulties in considering and distinguishing less popular freshwater fish can prompt testing predisposition — a peculiarity where certain animal types are overrepresented in examinations while others stay disregarded. This predisposition can result from variables like living space availability, scientist aptitude, or the perceivability of species, prompting a fragmented comprehension of the more extensive variety present inside freshwater biological systems.

Inclination for Magnetic Species: Analysts and financing offices might incline toward concentrating on alluring or monetarily important species, incidentally disregarding the biological meaning of less popular fish.

This inclination can propagate the misguided judgment that main outwardly striking or monetarily significant species warrant logical consideration.

Insufficient Examining Methods: The difficulties related with concentrating on slippery species might prompt the utilization of less designated testing strategies. Subsequently, certain environments or explicit ways of behaving might be underrepresented in examinations, making holes in how we might interpret the natural jobs and ways of behaving of less popular fish.

Mechanical Constraints: Devices for the Concealed

Progressions in innovation have without a doubt extended our capacities to concentrate on oceanic conditions, however mechanical limits persevere, impacting the profundity and accuracy of our perceptions.

Constraints of Submerged Cameras: While submerged cameras have become fundamental instruments for noticing oceanic life, they accompany impediments. Dinky waters, low-light circumstances, and complex environments can hinder the viability of regular submerged cameras. Scientists are constantly looking for headways, like better lighting frameworks and particular focal points, to defeat these difficulties.

Reliance on ROVs and Robots: In underground or testing conditions, analysts frequently go to remotely worked vehicles (ROVs) and drones for investigation. In any case, these apparatuses have their own arrangement of requirements, including battery duration, mobility, and restrictions in arriving at bound spaces. Mechanical development stays basic to upgrade the viability of these apparatuses in revealing the mysteries of stowed away living spaces.

Protection Suggestions: Supporting for the Inconspicuous

The difficulties in considering and recognizing less popular freshwater fish stretch out past the logical domain to have substantial protection suggestions. The frequently disregarded status of these species can bring about deficient protection measures, leaving them defenseless against the dangers confronting freshwater biological systems.

Restricted Preservation Consideration: Less popular fish species might get restricted consideration in protection plans contrasted with additional alluring or financially important species. This oversight can prompt inadequate security measures, allowing these species to be uncovered to living space obliteration, contamination, and overfishing.

Deficient Security of Stowed away Territories: The difficulties in getting to stowed away living spaces might add to an absence of understanding and, in this way, assurance for these conditions. Protection endeavors should address the particular requirements of less popular species and their living spaces to guarantee the conservation of the whole biological system.

Exploring Social Points of view: Overcoming any barrier

Social points of view on less popular freshwater fish can impact research needs, protection endeavors, and public mindfulness. Understanding and connecting these social holes is fundamental for successful correspondence and cooperation.

Social View of Fish Species: Certain societies might have explicit convictions, restrictions, or inclinations with respect to specific fish species. These social points of view can impact the prioritization of examination, preservation drives, and the use of fish assets. A nuanced comprehension of these social elements is essential for effective interdisciplinary coordinated effort.

Local area Commitment: By and large, nearby networks have significant information about the less popular fish species in their districts. Drawing in with these networks, regarding their social viewpoints, and coordinating native information into exploration and preservation endeavors can upgrade the viability of drives zeroed in on secret fortunes.

Chapter 2

The Diverse World of Lesser-Known Freshwater Fish

Ordered Variety
Prologue to Scientific classification
The scientific classification of less popular freshwater fish fills in as the primary part in our investigation. This part digs into the grouping, terminology, and developmental connections of these species. From the family and class levels to the complexities of species recognizable proof, we unwind the ordered riddle that characterizes the assorted universe of less popular fish.

Secretive Species and Morphological Varieties
A critical part of ordered variety is the presence of secretive species — those with comparative appearances yet unmistakable hereditary contrasts. We investigate how headways in sub-atomic strategies, including DNA barcoding, are fundamental for separating between these enigmatic species. Moreover, we dig into the difficulties presented by morphological varieties inside populaces, requiring a nuanced way to deal with grouping.

Geographic Conveyance and Endemism

The geographic dispersion of less popular freshwater fish is an embroidery woven across waterways, lakes, and wetlands around the world. This part investigates the elements affecting the circulation of these species, from verifiable cycles to natural transformations. The idea of endemism becomes the dominant focal point, underscoring the one of a kind animal categories tracked down in unambiguous geographic districts and the significance of protecting their territories.

Ways of behaving and Variations

Nighttime Ways of behaving and Systems for Endurance

Ways of behaving of less popular freshwater fish are in many cases molded by the difficulties of their surroundings. This part plunges into the nighttime ways of behaving showed by quite a few people of these species. From scavenging under the front of murkiness to sidestepping hunters, we unwind the procedures these fish utilize for endurance in their frequently tricky and dynamic natural surroundings.

Mimicry and Disguise

The flexibility of less popular fish reaches out to their actual qualities. Mimicry and cover assume urgent parts in their methods for surviving. This segment investigates the different types of mimicry, including Batesian and Müllerian mimicry, and how these variations empower fish to mix consistently into their environmental elements, staying away from identification by the two hunters and prey.

Specific Taking care of Propensities

The different universe of less popular freshwater fish incorporates species with profoundly specific taking care of propensities. From channel taking care of to base dwelling foragers, we reveal the complexities of how these species have developed to take advantage of explicit specialties inside their biological systems. The section features the environmental jobs played by these taking care of propensities and their commitments to supplement cycling.

Environment Variety

Secret Domains: Underground Living spaces

HIDDEN TREASURES

Certain less popular freshwater fish species occupy underground conditions, introducing a one of a kind domain for investigation. This section plunges into the difficulties and transformations related with life in underground living spaces. From cave-staying fish to those exploring underground streams, we disentangle the secrets of these hid environments.

Thick Vegetation and Distant Areas

Notwithstanding underground territories, less popular fish track down shelter in thickly vegetated regions or distant areas. This part investigates the variations that empower these fish to flourish in conditions like bogs, swamps, and segregated riverbanks. The difficulties specialists face in getting to these natural surroundings highlight the significance of creative examining methods.

Altitudinal Zonation and Its Effects

Freshwater environments show altitudinal zonation, with particular fish networks possessing various heights. This section investigates how less popular species adjust to changes in elevation, from marsh waterways to mountain streams. The effects of altitudinal zonation on the biodiversity and environment of these fish add to the general variety of freshwater biological systems.

Environmental Jobs and Cooperations

Biodiversity and Useful Variety

The environmental jobs of less popular freshwater fish are necessary to the general biodiversity and working of sea-going biological systems. This part investigates how these species add to useful variety, possessing explicit specialties that impact supplement cycling, prey-hunter elements, and the general flexibility of freshwater conditions.

Supplement Cycling and Environment Wellbeing

The multifaceted snare of life in freshwater biological systems depends on the commitments of less popular fish to supplement cycling. As bottom feeders upset dregs and channel feeders assume their parts, supplements are reused, supporting the efficiency of the biological

| 37 |

system. We dig into the interconnected connections that highlight the wellbeing and imperativeness of these oceanic conditions.

Hunter Prey Elements

Less popular fish partake in the sensitive dance of hunter prey elements, controlling populaces and keeping up with biological equilibrium. This segment investigates the methodologies utilized by these species as the two hunters and prey, stressing the significance of their jobs in forestalling the unrestrained expansion of specific creatures and supporting the general variety of freshwater environments.

Preservation Status and Difficulties

Restricted Protection Consideration

Regardless of their biological importance, numerous less popular freshwater fish species face difficulties originating from restricted protection consideration. This section investigates the elements adding to this oversight, from predispositions in research needs to the apparent absence of monetary worth in these species. The preservation status of different less popular fish and the dangers they experience are inspected, featuring the earnest requirement for protection measures.

Territory Obliteration and Contamination

The protection challenges looked by less popular freshwater fish reach out past disregard to incorporate substantial dangers to their environments. Environment obliteration, frequently determined by human exercises, and contamination present huge dangers to the endurance of these species. We investigate the effects of anthropogenic tensions and the flowing impacts on the general strength of freshwater environments.

Overfishing and Obtrusive Species

Notwithstanding territory dangers, overfishing and the presentation of obtrusive species arise as basic worries. The monetary and sporting worth of some less popular fish species can coincidentally prompt impractical fishing rehearses. At the same time, the presentation of non-local species can disturb existing environments, setting local fish in danger. This section tends to the intricacies of dealing with these difficulties and backers for practical protection techniques.

Innovative Advances and Cooperation
Submerged Cameras, ROVs, and Robots

Mechanical advances assume a significant part in disentangling the secrets of less popular freshwater fish. This part investigates how submerged cameras, remotely worked vehicles (ROVs), and drones give remarkable admittance to stowed away living spaces and ways of behaving. We dig into the abilities of these advancements and their commitments to extending how we might interpret the different world underneath the water's surface.

Natural DNA (eDNA) and Hereditary Investigations

In the domain of atomic nature, ecological DNA (eDNA) and hereditary examinations have reformed the investigation of less popular fish species. This segment investigates how these instruments empower specialists to identify and concentrate on species without direct perception. From uncovering the presence of species to unwinding their hereditary variety, we dig into the sub-atomic experiences that add to a thorough comprehension of these secret fortunes.

Social Importance and Native Information
Stories, Legends, and Customs

The investigation of less popular freshwater fish stretches out past logical request to include social aspects. This section explores the tales, legends, and customs related with these species. Native information, went down through ages, gives important bits of knowledge into the ways of behaving, natural jobs, and social meaning of less popular fish, advancing comprehension we might interpret their position on the planet.

Social Protection Practices

Understanding the social meaning of less popular fish species opens an entryway to investigating social preservation rehearses. This segment dives into how networks with rich social connections to these fish add to preservation endeavors. By regarding and coordinating native information, protection drives can be more all encompassing and successful in saving the variety of freshwater environments.

2.1 Overview of Different Families and Genera

In the immense and mind boggling universe of less popular freshwater fish, scientific categorization fills in as the guide through which researchers explore the intricacies of arrangement. This outline digs into different families and genera that add to the rich woven artwork of these frequently ignored oceanic occupants. From the assorted Cyprinidae to the mysterious Siluridae, every family and class discloses one of a kind qualities, ways of behaving, and biological jobs, enhancing how we might interpret the secret fortunes inside freshwater environments.

Cyprinidae: The Different Minnows and Carps

The Cyprinidae family remains as one of the most different and far and wide gatherings of freshwater fish. Involving more than 3,000 species, including minnows, carps, and points, Cyprinidae addresses a critical piece of the less popular oceanic occupants.

Minnows: Among the Cyprinidae, minnows frequently show a wonderful variety in size, shading, and living space inclinations. Going from the minute ruddy red minnow to the hearty brilliant shiner, these fish add to the biodiversity of waterways and streams around the world.

Carps and Spikes: Species like the normal carp and different points address the bigger and more hearty individuals from the Cyprinidae family. While some, similar to the koi carp, have acquired prevalence in fancy lakes, others stay concealed in the tranquil openings of freshwater environments.

Siluridae: The Puzzling Catfish

The Siluridae family, incorporating catfish species, adds a demeanor of secret to freshwater conditions. With their particular hair like barbels and frequently nighttime conduct, catfish typify the perplexing idea of less popular fish.

Channel Catfish: Broadly dispersed in North America, the channel catfish embodies the flexibility of Siluridae species. Perceived for its rummaging propensities, this catfish species assumes a crucial part in supplement cycling, adding to the environmental strength of its natural surroundings.

Glass Catfish: interestingly, the glass catfish, having a place with the Kryptopterus class, enamors spectators with its straightforward body. Local to Southeast Asia, this species explores the secret domains of waterways and streams, its clear appearance adding a component of interest to the freshwater scene.

Cichlidae: The Vivid Universe of Cichlids

Cichlids, a different family known for their dynamic tones and complex ways of behaving, address one more feature of less popular freshwater fish. With more than 1,600 species, they possess a scope of conditions from African lakes to South American streams.

African Cichlids: The cichlids of Africa's Fracture Valley lakes, for example, Lake Malawi and Lake Tanganyika, grandstand shocking varieties and complex social designs. From the gem cichlid to the electric yellow cichlid, these species explore the rough substrates and secret fissure of their natural surroundings.

South American Cichlids: In South America, the Apistogramma sort presents a different exhibit of cichlid species. Frequently found in calm, vegetated waters, these less popular fish add to the multifaceted mosaic of biodiversity in freshwater biological systems.

Gobiidae: The Multifaceted Universe of Gobies

Gobies, having a place with the Gobiidae family, comprise a gathering of little, frequently subtle fish that possess various sea-going conditions. Known for their versatility, gobies explore both freshwater and salty natural surroundings.

Honey bee Goby: The honey bee goby, delegate of the Brachygobius sort, epitomizes the captivating universe of Gobiidae. With its particular dark and yellow stripes, this minor fish frequently possesses freshwater streams and estuarine regions, displaying the versatility of gobies to differing saltiness levels.

Bantam Gobies: Various bantam goby species add to the biodiversity of freshwater living spaces, with individuals from the Pandaka and Stiphodon genera frequently staying in secret corners of streams and waterways. Their little size and secretive tinge mention them intriguing subjects for observable fact and study.

Pangasiidae: The Tricky Pangasiid Catfish

The Pangasiidae family presents the pangasiid catfish, a gathering that incorporates the famous Mekong goliath catfish. These less popular fish possess enormous streams and present exceptional difficulties and valuable open doors for protection endeavors.

Mekong Goliath Catfish: As one of the biggest freshwater fish internationally, the Mekong monster catfish achieves noteworthy sizes. Endemic to the Mekong Waterway bowl, this species exemplifies the difficulties related with moderating and concentrating on less popular fish, given its slippery nature and the immeasurability of its territory.

Balitoridae: The Variety of Hillstream Loaches

Hillstream loaches, having a place with the Balitoridae family, flourish in quick streaming streams and waterways, exhibiting variations to fierce conditions. These exceptional fish add to the biodiversity of freshwater living spaces with their specific attributes.

Butterfly Loach: Addressing the Schistura family, the butterfly loach is an illustration of the different transformations seen in Balitoridae species. With their straightened bodies and attractions cup-like mouths, these loaches grip to rocks in quick streaming streams, exploring the difficulties of their dynamic natural surroundings.

Hillstream Loach Variety: The more extensive variety of hillstream loaches, including genera like Sewellia and Gastromyzon, features the flexibility of Balitoridae species to changing stream conditions. Their presence in less popular freshwater natural surroundings adds to the general lavishness of amphibian life.

Centrarchidae: The Sunfish and Basses

Centrarchidae includes a gathering of freshwater fish known for their prevalence among fishers. The sunfish and basses, including species like the largemouth bass and bluegill, add to the sporting and biological elements of freshwater environments.

Largemouth Bass: Notorious in North American waters, the largemouth bass is eminent for its part in sporting fishing. Frequently concealed in lowered structures, these savage fish impact the elements of freshwater food networks.

Bluegill and Sunfish Variety: The bluegill and different sunfish species, like the pumpkinseed and longear sunfish, add variety to the Centrarchidae family. These less popular fish assume fundamental parts in adjusting oceanic populaces and add to the general strength of freshwater environments.

2.2 Unique Features and Adaptations

In the secret profundities of freshwater environments, less popular fish species unfurl an embroidery of exceptional highlights and transformations that recognize them from their more obvious partners. From secretive morphologies to particular ways of behaving, these fish explore a universe of difficulties and open doors, exhibiting their ability to surprise to flourish in different and frequently requesting conditions. This investigation dives into the unprecedented elements and transformations that spread the word about lesser freshwater fish genuine wonders of sea-going advancement.

Obscure Morphologies: The Craft of Mixing In
Straightforward Miracles: Glass Catfish (Kryptopterus class)

Quite possibly of the most outwardly striking transformation found in less popular freshwater fish is straightforwardness. The Glass Catfish, having a place with the Kryptopterus class, typifies this peculiarity. With an almost clear body, these fish appear to vanish into their sea-going environmental factors, making them tricky and confounding. This obscure variation fills in as a characteristic disguise, permitting them to explore clear streams and waterways while keeping away from according to hunters.

Mimicry Bosses: Butterfly Loach (Schistura class)

Mimicry is one more noteworthy component found in some less popular fish, and the Butterfly Loach of the Schistura variety is an expert of this workmanship. With designs looking like the wings of butterflies, these loaches mix flawlessly into the rough substrates of quick streaming streams. Mimicry fills both protective and ruthless needs, permitting them to sidestep hunters and trap clueless prey. The mind boggling dance of variety and example in the Butterfly Loach represents the versatility and cleverness of less popular fish.

Specific Ways of behaving: Exploring the Oceanic Labyrinth
Nighttime Pilots: Channel Catfish (Ictalurus punctatus)

Nighttime conduct is a typical transformation among less popular freshwater fish, giving an upper hand in the front of dimness. The Channel Catfish (Ictalurus punctatus) is a perfect representation, displaying uplifted action during evening time. This conduct permits them to scavenge for food and take part in conceptive exercises under the cloak of murkiness, keeping away from diurnal hunters and amplifying their possibilities of endurance.

Underground Voyagers: Blind Cavern Fish (Astyanax mexicanus)

In underground conditions, where light is a unique case, some less popular fish have developed to flourish in complete haziness. The Visually impaired Cavern Fish (Astyanax mexicanus) has lost its visual perception, depending on other tangible variations to explore underground streams and caverns. Improved material faculties and the capacity to identify unpretentious changes in water pressure empower these fish to investigate stowed away domains where conventional vision becomes outdated.

Physiological Transformations: Getting through in Different Conditions
Outrageous Strength: Killifish (Austrofundulus limnaeus)

Certain less popular fish show exceptional transformations to get through outrageous natural circumstances. The yearly Killifish (Austrofundulus limnaeus) faces the test of living in impermanent water bodies that might evaporate occasionally.

To defeat this, their incipient organisms can enter a condition of suspended liveliness, getting through parching until the following blustery season when the water returns. This remarkable variation features the versatility of less popular fish notwithstanding flighty natural surroundings.

Altitudinal Ability: Snow Trout (Schizothorax spp.)

In high-height streams and waterways, less popular fish feature transformations to adapt to bring down oxygen levels and colder temperatures. Snow Trout, having a place with the Schizothorax class, have specific hemoglobin that upgrades oxygen take-up in cool waters. Their smoothed out bodies and effective swimming skills empower them to explore the quick ebbs and flows of mountain streams, showing how physiological variations add to their progress in testing territories.

Regenerative Procedures: Guaranteeing Species Endurance

Mouthbrooding Dominance: Tanganyika Mouthbrooder (Tropheus spp.)

Regenerative procedures among less popular fish frequently include extraordinary ways of behaving that add to the endurance of their posterity. The Tanganyika Mouthbrooder, a cichlid of the Tropheus class, is known for mouthbrooding — a variation where the female conveys prepared eggs in her mouth until they hatch. This parental consideration gives a protected climate to the creating fry, safeguarding them from expected hunters and guaranteeing a higher opportunity of endurance.

Hazardous Generating: Breathtaking Darter (Etheostoma barrenense)

Some less popular fish utilize hazardous generating, a system where different people discharge eggs and sperm at the same time. The Astonishing Darter (Etheostoma barrenense), tracked down in North American streams, participates in this synchronized conceptive dance. By delivering eggs and sperm as one, these fish improve the probability of fruitful treatment and upgrade the hereditary variety of their populaces, adding to the versatility of the species.

Tactile Wonders: Exploring a Multisensory World

Electrolocation Specialists: Elephantnose Fish (Gnathonemus petersii)

In cloudy waters and low-perceivability conditions, some less popular fish depend on particular tactile transformations to explore and find prey. The Elephantnose Fish (Gnathonemus petersii) is an electrolocation master, utilizing electrical motivations to detect the general climate and recognize prey. This astounding transformation permits them to flourish in turbid waters, displaying the different techniques utilized by less popular fish to conquer natural difficulties.

Parallel Line Awareness: Hillstream Loaches (Variety Gastromyzon)

The parallel line, a tactile organ running at the edges of fish, assumes a critical part in recognizing changes in water strain and development. Hillstream Loaches, especially those of the Gastromyzon sort, use their exceptionally delicate parallel lines to explore quickly streaming streams. This transformation assists them with keeping up with position in tempestuous waters and stay away from snags, displaying the significance of tangible variations in less popular fish.

2.3 Geographical Distribution and Habitats

The universe of less popular freshwater fish is a tremendous embroidery woven across different geological scenes and natural surroundings. From the rambling waterway frameworks of the Amazon to the completely clear pools of East Africa, these fish explore different environments, each introducing remarkable difficulties and open doors for variation. This investigation digs into the topographical circulation and natural surroundings of less popular freshwater fish, uncovering the secret domains where these captivating species flourish.

Variety Across Mainlands: A Worldwide Odyssey

Amazon Bowl: Biodiversity Area of interest

The Amazon Bowl remains as an embodiment of biodiversity, facilitating a unimaginable cluster of less popular freshwater fish. From the unpredictably designed tetras to the obscure catfish, the Amazon's wandering waterways and overwhelmed woods give a different scope of living spaces. Inside this extensive bowl, less popular fish adjust to dynamic water levels, flourishing in overflowed regions during the blustery season and withdrawing to lowered woods as the waters retreat. The lavishness of the Amazon Bowl embodies the versatility of these fish to steadily evolving conditions.

African Fracture Lakes: Gem Cichlids and Then some

East African fracture lakes, including Lake Malawi and Lake Tanganyika, harbor a surprising variety of less popular fish, especially cichlids. The lively varieties and complex ways of behaving of gem cichlids make a one of a kind submerged display. These lakes, portrayed by their profound, clear waters and rough substrates, give specialties to particular transformations. Cichlids have developed to take advantage of different environmental specialties, bringing about a stunning exhibit of animal varieties that add to the biological intricacy of these break lake environments.

Southeast Asian Waterways: Gobies and Hillstream Loaches

The waterways of Southeast Asia, jumbling thick rainforests and rocky territories, have less popular fish like gobies and hillstream loaches.

Gobies, with their little size and obscure tinge, explore through the many-sided organization of waterways and streams. Hillstream loaches, adjusted to quick streaming waters, grip to rocks with pull cup-like mouths. The different scenes of Southeast Asia make a mosaic of territories, from marsh waterways to high-height streams, giving specialties to various less popular species.

North American Streams: Darters and Sunfish

The freshwater surges of North America are home to less popular species like darters and sunfish. Darters, with their energetic tones and unpredictable balance shows, occupy clear, streaming waters. Sunfish, including species like the longear sunfish, flourish in different living spaces, from sluggish streams to vegetated lakes. The calm environments of North America offer a scope of conditions where these fish display novel ways of behaving, adding to the biological variety of freshwater biological systems in the district.

Mekong Waterway Bowl: Pangasiid Catfish and the sky is the limit from there

The Mekong Waterway Bowl, flowing through Southeast Asia, harbors less popular species, including the famous Mekong monster catfish. Adjusted to the unique progression of the Mekong Waterway, these fish explore through lowered scenes and participate in broad movements. The bowl's assorted natural surroundings, from violent stream channels to disconnected feeders, grandstand the capacity of less popular fish to flourish in changed conditions. The protection of species like the Mekong goliath catfish features the interconnectedness of fish populaces inside this broad waterway framework.

Living space Specialization: Adjusting to Interesting Conditions

Underground Living spaces: Blind Cavern Fish and Mysterious Inhabitants

Some less popular fish have adjusted to underground conditions, where light is a unique case. The Visually impaired Cavern Fish, tracked down in underground streams and caverns, has developed to live in complete dimness, depending on other tactile variations for route. Obscure tenants, for example, cave-staying catfish, have particular morphologies that assist them with exploring the secret openings of underground living spaces. These transformations feature the flexibility of less popular fish in conditions where conventional obvious signals are missing.

Hillstream Conditions: Loaches and Their Quick Streaming Dwelling places

Hillstream loaches flourish in quick streaming streams with rough substrates, frequently described by fierce waters. Their smoothed out bodies and concentrated transformations, for example, solid pectoral balances, empower them to grip to rocks and explore the quick flows.

These fish, found in areas like Southeast Asia, feature the variety of territories less popular species possess and the novel morphological qualities that guide in their endurance in these powerful conditions.

Thick Vegetation: Exploring Bogs and Swamps

Certain less popular fish species possess thickly vegetated regions, like bogs and swamps, where exploring through thick vegetation is fundamental for endurance. Fish like the butterfly fish, adjusted to wind through oceanic plants, flourish in these detached living spaces. The thick vegetation gives both shelter and a rich wellspring of food, showing how less popular fish have developed to take advantage of explicit specialties inside their biological systems.

Altitudinal Zonation: Adjusting to Changing Heights

Freshwater biological systems show altitudinal zonation, with various fish species possessing explicit elevational ranges. Species like the Snow Trout, found in mountain streams at higher heights, feature transformations to colder temperatures and lower oxygen levels. The capacity of less popular fish to adjust to differing rises mirrors their versatility and ability to take advantage of assorted specialties inside freshwater environments.

Difficulties and Protection: Exploring Human Effects

Territory Obliteration: A Danger to Stowed away Domains

Human exercises, for example, deforestation and dam development, present huge dangers to the environments of less popular freshwater fish. The obliteration of lowered woods in waterway bowls like the Amazon decreases critical reproducing and scavenging grounds. Preservation endeavors should address territory annihilation and endeavor to safeguard the secret domains where these fish flourish, perceiving the interconnectedness of oceanic environments.

Contamination: Effect on Water Quality

Contamination, including horticultural spillover and modern releases, represents a danger to the water nature of freshwater territories. Less popular fish, frequently adjusted to explicit ecological circumstances, may experience the ill effects of poisons. From modified water science to the aggregation of poisons, contamination endangers the prosperity of these fish and the biological systems they possess. Protection drives should address the wellsprings of contamination and work towards saving water quality to support less popular species.

Overfishing: Adjusting Harvest and Preservation

A less popular fish animal categories face overfishing because of their monetary or sporting worth. Adjusting the gather of these species with protection measures is urgent for keeping up with solid populaces. Supportable fishing rehearses, combined with guidelines and local area commitment, assume a fundamental part in guaranteeing that overfishing doesn't drain populaces of less popular fish, protecting their natural jobs inside freshwater biological systems.

Intrusive Species: Upsetting Local Equilibrium

The presentation of non-local species can upset the fragile equilibrium of freshwater environments, affecting less popular fish and their natural surroundings. Obtrusive species may outcompete local fish for assets or present new sicknesses, presenting dangers to the biological respectability of amphibian conditions. Protection systems should address the control and avoidance of intrusive species to shield the one of a kind natural surroundings where less popular fish flourish.

Protection Techniques: Sustaining the Secret Fortunes

Natural surroundings Reclamation: Reconstructing Urgent Conditions

Natural surroundings reclamation assumes a fundamental part in moderating the different environments where less popular freshwater fish dwell. Endeavors to reestablish lowered woodlands, safeguard bringing forth grounds, and restore corrupted regions add to the protection of stowed away domains. Cooperative drives including neighborhood networks, scientists, and protection associations plan to modify significant conditions and give asylums to less popular fish.

Local area Commitment: Cultivating Stewardship

Connecting with neighborhood networks in protection endeavors is fundamental for the drawn out progress of saving less popular fish and their natural surroundings. Native information and customary practices frequently hold important experiences into the way of behaving and nature of these fish. By cultivating stewardship and including networks in observing and preservation programs, a comprehensive way to deal with safeguarding stowed away fortunes arises.

Examination and Checking: Uncovering Insider facts of Freshwater Biological systems

Logical exploration and observing drives are significant in divulging the mysteries of freshwater environments and the less popular fish inside them. Trend setting innovations, including natural DNA (eDNA) investigation and submerged cameras, give remarkable experiences into stowed away domains.

Long haul observing projects assist with following populace patterns, relocation designs, and the effects of human exercises, directing viable protection systems.

Strategy and Backing: Forming Protection Needs

Powerful preservation of less popular freshwater fish requires the detailing and execution of strategies that focus on the security of their territories. Backing endeavors at neighborhood, public, and global levels assume a vital part in forming protection needs. By bringing issues to light about the biological significance of these species and collecting support for defensive measures, policymakers can add to the maintainable concurrence of human exercises and the conservation of stowed away fortunes.

Chapter 3

The Ecological Significance

Freshwater biological systems, abounding with life underneath the surface, are multifaceted embroidered works of art of interconnected connections. Inside this domain, less popular freshwater fish arise as quiet overseers, contributing altogether to the natural agreement that supports the equilibrium of amphibian life. This investigation digs into the significant biological meaning of these frequently disregarded species, unwinding the jobs they play in supplement cycling, hunter prey elements, living space support, and the general versatility of freshwater conditions.

Biodiversity and Practical Variety
1.1 The Mosaic of Biodiversity

The environmental meaning of less popular freshwater fish starts with the extravagance of biodiversity they bring to amphibian biological systems. While famous species might rule the spotlight, the mosaic of less popular fish adds profundity and intricacy. Various families, genera, and species make a powerful local area where every part assumes a remarkable part, adding to the general wellbeing and flexibility of the biological system.

1.2 Useful Variety and Specialty Inhabitance

Past sheer numbers, the useful variety of less popular fish is a foundation of their biological importance. These species possess explicit biological specialties, each with a bunch of jobs and obligations. From base dwelling catfish that upset dregs to channel taking care of minnows that add to water clearness, the utilitarian variety of less popular fish is a demonstration of their flexibility and the perplexing trap of connections that supports freshwater biological systems.

Supplement Cycling and Biological system Wellbeing

2.1 The Gatekeepers of Supplement Cycling

Less popular freshwater fish arise as gatekeepers of supplement cycling, effectively partaking in the reusing of natural matter inside oceanic biological systems. Base dwelling species, like catfish and loaches, upset dregs during scrounging, delivering supplements once more into the water. Channel feeders, including specific minnows and goby species, assume a significant part in keeping up with water clearness while adding to supplement cycling. The multifaceted dance of supplement trade arranged by these fish cultivates the wellbeing and efficiency of freshwater conditions.

2.2 Supporting Biological system Efficiency

Supplement cycling, worked with by less popular fish, is fundamental for supporting biological system efficiency. As these fish add to the disintegration of natural matter, supplements are made accessible to sea-going plants and phytoplankton. Thusly, this supports the groundwork of the freshwater food web, guaranteeing a ceaseless stockpile of assets for a horde of creatures, from tiny green growth to bigger fish and spineless creatures.

Hunter Prey Elements

3.1 Adjusting Populaces

Less popular freshwater fish assume a crucial part in controlling populaces through complex hunter prey elements. As the two hunters and prey, they add to the sensitive equilibrium that forestalls uncontrolled expansion of specific species. For example, ruthless fish hold in line the populaces of more modest fish and spineless creatures, forestalling overgrazing and keeping a different gathering of animal categories inside freshwater biological systems.

3.2 Trophic Fountains and Biotic Control

The environmental meaning of less popular fish reaches out to trophic fountains — roundabout impacts that engender through the food web. By affecting the overflow and conduct of their prey, these fish apply biotic command over lower trophic levels. This guideline has flowing consequences for the whole environment, forestalling the predominance of specific species and cultivating biodiversity inside freshwater living spaces.

Environment Support and Underlying Intricacy

4.1 Making Concealing Spots and Generating Grounds

The ways of behaving of less popular freshwater fish add to natural surroundings support and the formation of primary intricacy inside amphibian conditions. Certain species participate in digging and tunneling exercises, making concealing spots for them and different creatures. These submerged designs act as safe houses for more modest fish, spineless creatures, and the posterity of different species, improving the general biodiversity of freshwater environments.

4.2 Supporting Microhabitats

The meaning of less popular fish lies in their capacity to support microhabitats inside bigger biological systems. Gobies, for instance, may make sorrows in the substrate that act as homes for their eggs. These microhabitats offer shelter for creating undeveloped organisms and add to the in general regenerative progress of these species.

The unpredictable ways of behaving of less popular fish encourage the production of assorted specialties, supporting the endurance and development of different amphibian creatures.

Variations to Ecological Changes

5.1 Flexibility Despite Ecological Fluctuation

Less popular freshwater fish exhibit versatility to ecological changes, adding to the flexibility of freshwater environments. Their capacity to explore through shifting water levels, temperature vacillations, and natural surroundings adjustments empowers them to flourish in powerful conditions. As sentinels of progress, these fish give bits of knowledge into the soundness of sea-going biological systems and their ability to endure normal and anthropogenic unsettling influences.

5.2 Pointer Species for Biological system Wellbeing

Certain less popular fish species capability as pointer species, mirroring the general wellbeing and state of freshwater biological systems. Changes in their overflow, conduct, or conceptive examples can flag shifts in ecological circumstances. Checking these species gives significant data to surveying the effect of human exercises, environmental change, and contamination on the biological uprightness of sea-going conditions.

Social and Sporting Worth

6.1 Social Associations with Less popular Fish

The environmental meaning of less popular freshwater fish reaches out past logical domains to social associations. In numerous networks, these fish hold social and customary significance. Native information frequently perceives the natural jobs of these species, encouraging a comprehensive comprehension of their importance inside the more extensive social embroidery.

6.2 Sporting Open doors and Ecotourism

Certain less popular fish, valued for their remarkable attributes or wearing characteristics, add to sporting open doors and ecotourism. Fishers and aficionados search out these secret fortunes, increasing the value of their preservation. The enthusiasm for the environmental jobs of these fish interlaces with sporting pursuits, making a scaffold among preservation and human commitment with freshwater biological systems.

Protection Difficulties and Systems

7.1 Overexploitation and Unreasonable Practices

Notwithstanding their environmental importance, less popular freshwater fish face various protection challenges. Overexploitation because of impractical fishing rehearses, territory obliteration, and the presentation of obtrusive species compromise the sensitive equilibrium these fish help keep up with. Protection endeavors should address these difficulties to guarantee the drawn out endurance of less popular species and the soundness of freshwater biological systems.

7.2 Local area Based Preservation and Support

Local area based preservation drives, established in nearby information and commitment, are urgent in protecting the natural meaning of less popular freshwater fish. Engaging people group to become stewards of their oceanic surroundings cultivates a feeling of obligation and coordinated effort. Promotion at nearby, local, and worldwide levels enhances the voices requiring the insurance of these frequently neglected species and their environments.

7.3 Incorporating Science, Strategy, and Public Mindfulness

A complete way to deal with preservation includes the combination of science, strategy, and public mindfulness. Logical examination reveals the secrets of less popular fish, giving an establishment to confirm based strategies. Public mindfulness crusades make a more extensive comprehension of the natural jobs these fish play, collecting support for protection drives. The collaboration of these components adds to viable preservation procedures that support the environmental meaning of less popular freshwater fish.

3.1 Lesser-Known Fish in Food Chains

Inside the complicated trap of freshwater biological systems, less popular fish assume crucial parts in the complex and frequently covered up show of well established pecking orders. While the spotlight frequently beams on bigger, more notable species, these secret fortunes act as fundamental connections interfacing the different levels of the oceanic food web. This investigation digs into the nuanced jobs less popular fish play in pecking orders, from their situation as prey and hunters to their effect on supplement cycling and by and large environment elements.

1. **The Less popular Fish as Prey: Sustaining the Sea-going Domain**

   1.1 The Menu for Hunters

   In freshwater natural pecking orders, less popular fish frequently end up on the menu for a different exhibit of hunters. From piscivorous birds like herons and kingfishers to bigger fish species, these prey fish structure a basic connection in the exchange of energy through the environment.

   Their overflow and dietary benefit make them a significant food hotspot for hunters, supporting the higher trophic levels inside the pecking order.

   1.2 The Back-and-forth: Adjusting Prey Populaces

   The predation on less popular fish serves a significant job in adjusting prey populaces. Hunters assist with controlling the wealth of more modest fish, forestalling unrestrained populace development that could prompt overgrazing of sea-going vegetation and consumption of assets. This fragile back-and-forth among hunters and prey adds to the general wellbeing and biodiversity of freshwater biological systems.

2. **Savage Jobs of Less popular Fish: Keeping up with Environmental Amicability**

   2.1 The Snare Specialists: Ruthless Ways of behaving

   Certain less popular fish species embrace ruthless ways of behaving, filling in as trap hunters or effectively chasing after more modest prey. For instance, savage minnows might lie on pause among sea-going vegetation, prepared to strike at passing spineless creatures or more modest fish. These savage jobs add to the guideline of prey populaces and keep a different collection of animal types inside freshwater environments.

   2.2 Trophic Outpouring Impacts: Affecting Lower Trophic Levels

   The ruthless jobs of less popular fish reach out past their nearby effect on prey populaces. Through trophic fountains, these hunters impact lower trophic levels in the established pecking order. By controlling the wealth of specific prey species, they in a roundabout way shape the elements of essential makers and different living beings inside the biological system. This perplexing dance of hunter prey associations adds to the biological equilibrium of freshwater pecking orders.

3. **Less popular Fish in Supplement Cycling: Concealed Draftsmen of Environment Efficiency**

   3.1 Foragers and Dregs Disturbers

   Certain less popular fish species add to supplement cycling by searching and upsetting dregs. Base dwelling fish, including catfish and loaches, effectively upset the substrate during taking care of. This interaction discharges supplements caught in the dregs, adding to the cycling of natural matter inside the environment. The exercises of these foragers assume an essential part in keeping up with supplement balance and advancing biological system efficiency.

   3.2 Channel Feeders: Lucidity and Supplement Cycling

   Some less popular fish, like specific minnows and gobies, are capable channel feeders. By extricating suspended particles from the water section, they add to water clearness while at the same time partaking in supplement cycling. These channel taking care of ways of behaving improve the general soundness of freshwater biological systems by forestalling inordinate turbidity and advancing the effective cycling of supplements.

4. **The Effect of Less popular Fish on Invertebrate Populaces**

   4.1 Invertebrate Prey: A Dietary Staple

   Spineless creatures, going from bugs to sea-going hatchlings, structure a huge part of the eating routine for some less popular fish species. These spineless creatures act as a dietary staple, giving fundamental supplements to the development and multiplication of the fish. The predation on spineless creatures by less popular fish adds to the guideline of invertebrate populaces, forestalling episodes that could prompt irregular characteristics inside the biological system.

4.2 Biotic Control: Impacting Invertebrate Way of behaving

The presence of less popular fish in freshwater pecking orders impacts the way of behaving and conveyance of spineless creatures. The apprehension about predation prompts spineless creatures to adjust their taking care of and conceptive ways of behaving, staying away from regions visited by fish. This biotic control applied by less popular fish adds to the spatial appropriation and wealth of invertebrate populaces, molding the general construction of freshwater biological systems.

5. Less popular Fish as Connecting Species: Interfacing Trophic Levels

5.1 Connecting Holes in the Food Web

Less popular fish act as pivotal connecting species, interfacing different trophic levels inside freshwater food networks. As the two hunters and prey, they work with the exchange of energy and supplements among lower and higher trophic levels. This interconnectedness upgrades the security and strength of the whole food web, guaranteeing the effective progression of energy through different levels of the biological system.

5.2 Cornerstone Species: Influencing Biological system Design

In specific cases, less popular fish might work as cornerstone species, applying a lopsided impact on the construction and elements of freshwater biological systems. Their exercises, whether as hunters or supplement cyclers, have flowing impacts that resound through the whole food web. Perceiving the cornerstone jobs of these fish is critical for understanding and rationing the complex equilibrium they bring to sea-going conditions.

6. Difficulties to Less popular Fish in Pecking orders: Protection Goals

6.1 Overfishing and Impractical Practices

Regardless of their natural importance, less popular fish face dangers from overfishing and unreasonable fishing rehearses. The interest for specific species in nearby and worldwide business sectors, frequently determined by their exceptional qualities or customary purposes, can prompt populace declines. Protection endeavors should address these difficulties to guarantee the proceeded with presence of less popular fish in freshwater natural pecking orders.

6.2 Living space Obliteration and Changed Conditions

Natural surroundings obliteration, coming about because of exercises like deforestation, dam development, and urbanization, represents a critical danger to the environments of less popular fish. Modified conditions might disturb the fragile equilibrium of hunter prey associations, supplement cycling, and generally speaking biological system elements. Preservation methodologies should focus on natural surroundings assurance and reclamation to shield the jobs these fish play in freshwater well established pecking orders.

6.3 Environmental Change Effects

Environmental change acquaints extra difficulties with less popular fish in freshwater pecking orders. Adjusted temperature systems, changes in precipitation examples, and changes in natural surroundings accessibility can affect the conveyance and conduct of these fish. Preservation endeavors should integrate environment strength procedures to address the unique difficulties presented by an evolving environment.

7. Preservation Techniques: Saving the Strings of Freshwater Food Networks

7.1 Maintainable Fishing Practices

Advancing maintainable fishing rehearses is fundamental for the preservation of less popular fish in freshwater established pecking orders. Executing get limits, size guidelines, and occasional terminations assist with forestalling overexploitation and permit fish populaces to recharge. Local area based approaches that include nearby partners in practical asset the board add to the drawn out wellbeing of oceanic environments.

7.2 Territory Assurance and Reclamation

Preservation drives should focus on the insurance and rebuilding of environments basic to less popular fish. This incorporates protecting generating grounds, keeping up with vegetated regions, and defending the different microhabitats these fish depend on. Natural surroundings rebuilding projects add to the strength of freshwater biological systems and backing the many-sided jobs less popular fish play in pecking orders.

7.3 Training and Mindfulness

Bringing issues to light about the natural meaning of less popular fish is vital for their protection. Training programs, focused on at both neighborhood networks and more extensive crowds, cultivate a comprehension of the jobs these fish play in freshwater natural pecking orders. Appreciation for the interconnectedness of oceanic environments supports mindful stewardship and preservation rehearses.

7.4 Exploration and Checking

Logical exploration and checking drives are imperative for disentangling the intricacies of freshwater natural pecking orders including less popular fish. Consistent checking helps track populace patterns, ways of behaving, and reactions to ecological changes. Coordinating examination discoveries into preservation procedures guarantees that administration rehearses are educated by a strong comprehension regarding the environmental jobs of these fish.

3.2 Niche Specialization and Interactions

In the secret domains of freshwater biological systems, less popular fish participate in a dance of specialty specialization and communications, winding around an embroidery of natural complexities that shape the elements of their surroundings. Specialty specialization alludes to the remarkable jobs and variations that species create to possess explicit biological specialties, while cooperations envelop the bunch ways these species draw in with one another and their environmental factors. This investigation digs into the nuanced universe of specialty specialization and communications among less popular freshwater fish, unwinding the strings that add to the variety, versatility, and equilibrium of amphibian environments.

1. **Specialty Specialization: Adjusting to Exceptional Jobs**
   1.1 The Mosaic of Living spaces and Jobs
   Freshwater conditions are portrayed by a mosaic of natural surroundings, each introducing particular difficulties and open doors. Less popular fish have developed to involve explicit environmental specialties inside these living spaces, displaying an exceptional exhibit of specialty specialization. From the base dwelling catfish that filter through residue to the surface-staying hatchetfish adjusted for life close to the water's surface, these species have sharpened their transformations to flourish specifically specialties.

   1.2 Trophic Specialties: Disentangling Taking care of Procedures
   Trophic specialties, characterized by an organic entity's situation in the established pecking order and its taking care of propensities, represent the variety of specialty specialization among less popular fish.
   A few animal groups, as ruthless minnows, involve the upper trophic levels, effectively hunting more modest fish and spineless creatures. Conversely, herbivorous fish, like specific carp species, represent considerable authority in benefiting from amphibian vegetation, adding to supplement cycling and natural surroundings support. The complicated snare of trophic specialties mirrors the versatile variety that less popular fish bring to freshwater biological systems.

2. **Conduct Transformations: The Specialty of Endurance**
   2.1 Nighttime Methodologies: Secret In obscurity
   Numerous less popular fish show social variations, like nighttime

exercises, to expand their possibilities of endurance. Nighttime species, similar to specific catfish and loaches, explore through the waters under the front of murkiness, staying away from diurnal hunters. This conduct specialization permits them to take advantage of explicit specialties and assets during the evening time, exhibiting the variety of procedures these fish utilize to flourish in their surroundings.

2.2 Social Designs: From Isolation to Tutoring

The social designs of less popular fish change generally, from single species to those that structure perplexing schools or reefs. A few animal varieties, similar to tetras, find security in larger groups, shaping huge schools that befuddle hunters and upgrade scrounging productivity. Conversely, certain cichlids might lay out domains and show complex social ways of behaving connected with multiplication and protection. These social transformations feature the variety of specialty specialization in light of various natural tensions.

3. Specialty Cross-over: Difficult exercise in Shared Spaces

3.1 The Crossing point of Specialties

In the interconnected universe of freshwater biological systems, specialty cross-over happens when various species share comparative natural specialties. This can prompt rivalry for assets, and less popular fish have advanced different techniques to explore this difficult exercise. A few animal varieties might parcel assets by using different microhabitats or taking care of at various times, lessening direct contest. Specialty cross-over cultivates mind boggling biological connections and shapes the concurrence of species inside shared spaces.

3.2 Asset Dividing: Tracking down Concordance in Variety

Asset parceling is a component by which animal categories with covering specialties partition accessible assets to decrease contest. Less popular fish might show asset apportioning in viewpoints like eating regimen, territory use, or taking care of conduct.

For instance, various types of catfish in a similar biological system might parcel food assets by focusing on various prey things or using unmistakable searching techniques. Asset parceling adds to the variety of species inside a local area and advances environmental concordance.

4. **Cooperations in Rearing and Regenerative Procedures**

    4.1 Rearing Specialties: Guaranteeing Posterity Endurance

    Rearing and conceptive techniques are key parts of specialty specialization among less popular fish. Species might display inclinations for explicit rearing environments, for example, rock beds, lowered vegetation, or rough cleft. The choice of rearing specialties guarantees appropriate circumstances for egg statement and gives assurance to posterity. The variety in rearing procedures adds to the by and large regenerative achievement and populace elements of these fish.

    4.2 Parental Consideration: Sustaining the Future

    Parental consideration ways of behaving, going from home structure to the guard of eggs and sear, grandstand the variety of regenerative specialty specialization. A few animal groups, similar to specific cichlids, put essentially in parental consideration, effectively watching and keeping an eye on their posterity. Interestingly, different species might take on a transmission producing technique, delivering eggs and sperm into the water with negligible parental contribution. These conceptive collaborations add to the endurance and enrollment of new ages inside freshwater environments.

5. **The Job of Contest and Participation**

    5.1 Intraspecific and Interspecific Contest

    Contest is a main impetus in the specialty elements of less popular fish. Intraspecific contest happens among people of similar species, while interspecific rivalry includes cooperations between various species competing for comparable assets. Less popular fish have developed different variations, including regional ways of behaving, rummaging techniques, and natural surroundings inclinations, to relieve the impacts of rivalry and coincide inside shared conditions.

5.2 Mutualistic Connections: Collaboration for Endurance

Helpful connections likewise assume a part in the elements of less popular fish networks. Mutualistic connections, where various species benefit from one another, add to the general strength of freshwater environments. For instance, certain cleaner fish might shape cooperative associations with bigger fish, eliminating parasites and dead tissue. These mutualistic collaborations grandstand the interconnected idea of specialty specialization and participation among less popular fish.

6. Difficulties to Specialty Specialization and Connections: Human Effects

6.1 Natural surroundings Obliteration: Upsetting Specialties and Connections

Human exercises, like deforestation, urbanization, and dam development, present critical dangers to the territories of less popular fish. Living space obliteration upsets the unpredictable specialties these fish have advanced to possess, prompting environment debasement and fracture. The deficiency of basic rearing and rummaging grounds can influence conceptive achievement and change the communications between species, endangering the fragile equilibrium of freshwater environments.

6.2 Obtrusive Species: Modifying Specialty Elements

The presentation of non-local species represents a danger to the specialty elements and connections of less popular fish. Intrusive species may outcompete local fish for assets, adjust natural surroundings structure, or present new sicknesses. These disturbances can prompt changes in specialty specialization, serious orders, and generally local area piece, presenting difficulties to the endurance of local species.

6.3 Environmental Change: Moving Biological Setting

Environmental change acquaints dynamic difficulties with specialty specialization and connections among less popular fish. Changes in temperature, precipitation examples, and natural surroundings accessibility can affect the dispersion and conduct of these fish. Changes in biological settings might prompt adjustments in taking care of propensities, rearing ways of behaving, and the planning of basic life cycle occasions. Transformation to a changing environment turns into a basic consider keeping up with the biological equilibrium of freshwater environments.

7. **Protection Procedures: Saving Specialty Variety and Communications**

7.1 Natural surroundings Insurance and Rebuilding

Preservation endeavors should focus on the assurance and reclamation of basic territories for less popular fish. Safeguarding assorted microhabitats, favorable places, and scavenging regions is fundamental for keeping up with specialty variety and supporting the connections that add to biological system versatility. Natural surroundings reclamation undertakings can relieve the effects of human-incited environment obliteration, encouraging the circumstances for specialty specialization and cooperations to flourish.

7.2 Obtrusive Species The board

Overseeing and forestalling the spread of intrusive species is vital for protecting the specialty elements of freshwater biological systems. Control measures, for example, the expulsion of intrusive species and the rebuilding of local living spaces, assist with relieving the disturbances brought about by non-local contenders.

Proactive systems to forestall the presentation of obtrusive species, including severe biosecurity measures, are fundamental for keeping up with the respectability of specialty associations.

7.3 Environment Tough Preservation Systems

Protection procedures should coordinate environment flexibility to address the difficulties presented by an evolving environment. This incorporates observing the effects of environmental change on the dissemination and ways of behaving of less popular fish, executing versatile administration rehearses, and advancing territory hallways that consider regular relocation in light of moving ecological circumstances. Environment strong protection guarantees the drawn out endurance of specialty specialization and communications inside freshwater biological systems.

7.4 Local area Commitment and Schooling

Including neighborhood networks in preservation endeavors is critical to the progress of protecting specialty specialization and collaborations among less popular fish. Local area commitment cultivates a comprehension of the biological significance of these species and empowers feasible practices. Training programs that feature the complex dance of specialty elements and connections advance a feeling of stewardship, engaging networks to add to the protection of freshwater environments.

3.3 Conservation Concerns and Threats

The secret fortunes of freshwater biological systems, less popular fish, face a bunch of protection concerns and dangers that cast shadows on the fragile equilibrium of their environments. As caretakers of these sea-going domains, our obligation is to disentangle the intricacies that endanger these frequently neglected species. This investigation dives into the protection concerns and dangers that loom over less popular freshwater fish, from territory corruption and contamination to overexploitation and the effects of environmental change.

1. **Natural surroundings Corruption: The Disintegration of Home**
   ### 1.1 Deforestation and Waterway Adjustment
   One of the essential protection worries for less popular freshwater fish is territory debasement coming about because of deforestation and adjustments to stream frameworks. Deforestation along riverbanks reduces the fundamental cushion zones that safeguard

amphibian environments from sedimentation, supplement spillover, and temperature variances. Changes in stream because of dams and channelization further disturb living spaces, affecting the accessibility of critical reproducing and scrounging grounds.

1.2 Discontinuity and Loss of Availability

Human exercises, like the development of dams and streets, section freshwater natural surroundings, detaching populaces of less popular fish. Environment discontinuity hinders normal relocation designs, influencing the capacity of fish to get to rearing destinations or find reasonable searching regions. The deficiency of network reduces hereditary variety and versatility inside populaces, making them more defenseless against natural changes.

2. **Contamination: Polluted Waters and Changed Conditions**

   2.1 Horticultural Spillover and Supplement Contamination

   Horticultural spillover presents abundance supplements, pesticides, and herbicides into freshwater environments, prompting supplement contamination. Less popular fish, adjusted to explicit ecological circumstances, may battle to adapt to changed water science. Supplement irregular characteristics can fuel algal blossoms, exhaust oxygen levels, and upset the fragile natural equilibrium whereupon these fish depend.

   2.2 Modern Releases and Poisons

   Modern exercises add to contamination through the arrival of harmful substances into freshwater environments. Less popular fish, frequently accomplished in their aversion to water quality, may experience the ill effects of impurities. From weighty metals to modern synthetic compounds, the collection of poisons can hinder the wellbeing and regenerative outcome of these fish, presenting huge dangers to their populaces.

3. **Overexploitation: Unreasonable Reaping Practices**

   3.1 Monetary and Sporting Tensions

   A less popular fish face overexploitation because of their monetary or sporting worth. The interest for these species in nearby and worldwide business sectors, driven by their remarkable attributes or customary purposes, comes down on populaces. Overfishing can drain stocks, disturb conceptive cycles, and lead to the decay of less popular fish species, endangering their natural jobs inside freshwater biological systems.

3.2 Bycatch and Potentially negative side-effects

Potentially negative side-effects of fishing rehearses, like bycatch, further add to overexploitation. Less popular fish got unexpectedly in fishing gear planned for different species might confront populace declines without direct focusing on. Bycatch can present irregular characteristics in the food web and influence the collaborations between less popular fish and their prey or hunters, enhancing protection concerns.

4. Intrusive Species: Upsetting Local Congruity

4.1 Presentation of Non-Local Contenders

The presentation of non-local species represents a huge danger to the sensitive equilibrium of freshwater biological systems. Obtrusive species, whether deliberate or inadvertent presentations, can outcompete local less popular fish for assets. This opposition changes the elements of environmental specialties, prompting decreases in local populaces and possibly causing flowing impacts all through the whole biological system.

4.2 Predation and Illness Presentation

Obtrusive species may likewise acquaint new hunters or infections with freshwater natural surroundings. Less popular fish, frequently adjusted to explicit hunter prey connections and infection conditions, may need guards against these clever dangers. The presentation of intrusive species disturbs the regular cooperations between less popular fish and their current circumstance, presenting difficulties to their endurance and the soundness of freshwater environments.

5. Environmental Change Effects: Moving Flows of Presence

5.1 Changed Temperature Systems

Environmental change achieves shifts in temperature systems, influencing the warm inclinations and resistances of less popular fish. Species adjusted to explicit temperature reaches might confront difficulties in adapting to hotter or cooler waters. Changes in temperature can affect conceptive achievement, taking care of ways of behaving, and generally physiological capabilities, modifying the communications between less popular fish and their current circumstance.

5.2 Environment Alterations and Water Level Vacillations

The effects of environmental change reach out to natural surroundings adjustments and vacillations in water levels. Less popular fish, adjusted to explicit territory designs and occasional varieties, may battle to explore changed conditions. Changes in precipitation examples and water levels can affect the accessibility of basic rearing and scavenging grounds, upsetting the unpredictable equilibrium these fish add to freshwater environments.

6. Preservation Systems: Sustaining the Secret Gatekeepers

6.1 Territory Assurance and Reclamation

Protecting and reestablishing basic environments is a foundation of preservation methodologies for less popular freshwater fish. Endeavors to safeguard riverbanks, keep up with vegetated regions, and restore corrupted territories add to the strength and prosperity of these fish.

Natural surroundings reclamation projects assume an imperative part in guaranteeing that reproducing and searching grounds stay in one piece, giving safe-havens to the secret watchmen of freshwater environments.

6.2 Maintainable Fishing Practices and Guideline

Advancing maintainable fishing rehearses is fundamental for moderating the effects of overexploitation. Carrying out guidelines, for example, get limits, size limitations, and occasional terminations, forestalls the exhaustion of less popular fish populaces. Drawing in with neighborhood networks and fishers to embrace reasonable practices cultivates a harmony among gathering and protection, guaranteeing the proceeded with presence of these fish in freshwater environments.

6.3 Obtrusive Species The board and Avoidance

Overseeing and forestalling the spread of intrusive species is essential for protecting the local congruity of freshwater biological systems. Methodologies might incorporate the expulsion of obtrusive species, checking and early discovery programs, and the execution of severe biosecurity measures. By tending to the underlying drivers of obtrusive species presentations, preservation endeavors mean to defend the cooperations and biological jobs of less popular fish.

6.4 Water Quality Checking and Contamination Anticipation

Checking and further developing water quality are fundamental parts of preservation techniques. Ordinary evaluations of water science, contamination levels, and natural surroundings conditions give important experiences into the strength of freshwater environments. Contamination avoidance measures, like diminishing supplement spillover and managing modern releases, add to keeping up with the immaculate circumstances essential for the endurance of less popular fish.

6.5 Environment Strong Preservation

Incorporating environment flexibility into protection techniques is pivotal for tending to the unique difficulties presented by environmental change. This incorporates observing the effects of environmental change on less popular fish populaces, carrying out versatile administration practices, and supporting living space reclamation projects that upgrade the flexibility of freshwater biological systems. Environment versatile protection guarantees the versatile limit of less popular fish even with changing natural circumstances.

Chapter 4

Fascinating Behaviors

In the perplexing dance of freshwater environments, less popular fish play out an ensemble of ways of behaving that frequently get away from the spotlight. These ways of behaving, formed by developmental transformations and natural tensions, add to the versatility, variety, and equilibrium of oceanic conditions. This investigation digs into the intriguing ways of behaving showed by less popular freshwater fish, from multifaceted mating customs and helpful systems to novel taking care of propensities and transient excursions.

1. Presentation: The Secret Universe of Conduct in Freshwater Fish

In the secret domains underneath the water's surface, the ways of behaving of less popular freshwater fish weave an embroidery of variations and cooperations. As eyewitnesses of this oceanic expressive dance, we leave on an excursion to disentangle the intricacies that shape the existences of these frequently disregarded species. From the profundities of their living spaces to the shallows of their favorable places, the ways of behaving of less popular fish uncover the nuanced methodologies they utilize for endurance, multiplication, and route in the powerful scenes of freshwater biological systems.

2. Taking care of Ways of behaving: Exploring the Smorgasbord of Sea-going Life

2.1 Specialty Specialization in Taking care of

Less popular freshwater fish show a striking variety in taking care of ways of behaving, frequently particular to take advantage of explicit specialties inside their territories. From base dwelling catfish that filter through dregs for spineless creatures to surface-taking care of hatchetfish that grab bugs from the air, these ways of behaving feature the versatile techniques these fish utilize to get their feasts. Understanding the complexities of their taking care of ways of behaving gives bits of knowledge into the jobs they play in supplement cycling and the general soundness of freshwater environments.

2.2 Channel Taking care of and Micropredation

Certain less popular fish species have developed interesting taking care of procedures, for example, channel taking care of and micropredation. Channel feeders, similar to certain minnows and gobies, remove suspended particles from the water section, adding to water lucidity and supplement cycling. Micropredators, then again, target small spineless creatures and hatchlings, displaying the differed approaches these fish take to meet their dietary requirements.

The investigation of their taking care of ways of behaving discloses the assorted biological jobs they play inside freshwater food networks.

**3. Conceptive Ceremonies: Dance, Show, and Commitment

3.1 Mind boggling Mating Ceremonies

Conceptive ways of behaving among less popular freshwater fish are frequently mind boggling and species-explicit. Mating customs might include elaborate romance presentations, lively hues, or synchronized developments. These customs fill numerous needs, from drawing in likely mates to laying out progressive strength inside reproducing populaces. Looking at the subtleties of mating ways of behaving gives a brief look into the conceptive methodologies that add to the achievement and variety of these fish populaces.

3.2 Home Structure and Parental Consideration

Some less popular fish take part in home structure ways of behaving as a component of their regenerative customs. This might include making structures from plant materials, unearthing pits in the substrate, or utilizing extraordinarily planned homes. Moreover, certain species show exceptional parental consideration, with one or the two guardians effectively having a tendency to eggs and sear. The devotion of these fish to guaranteeing the endurance of their posterity adds layers of intricacy to the social woven artwork of freshwater biological systems.

**4. Social Designs: From Isolation to Sandbars

4.1 Singular Propensities and Territoriality

While some less popular fish favor single ways of life, laying out and safeguarding domains, others structure multifaceted social designs. Regional ways of behaving, set apart by the protection of explicit regions for taking care of or rearing, add to the spatial dispersion and biological elements of these species. Understanding the elements affecting territoriality gives experiences into the systems less popular fish utilize to augment their admittance to assets and regenerative open doors.

4.2 Tutoring and Agreeable Procedures

Interestingly, numerous less popular fish structure schools or reefs, where people coordinate their developments for different advantages. Tutoring gives security from hunters, improves searching proficiency, and helps in route. Helpful ways of behaving inside schools might incorporate composed hunting, hunter avoidance strategies, or synchronized producing. The investigation of these social designs discloses the cooperative procedures that less popular fish utilize for endurance and variation in their oceanic surroundings.

**5. Nighttime Ways of behaving: Flourishing in the Shadows

5.1 Transformations to Nighttime Life

Numerous less popular freshwater fish show nighttime ways of behaving, exploring and rummaging under the front of murkiness. Nighttime transformations might incorporate specific tactile organs, changes in shading, or adjusted movement designs. These ways of behaving permit fish to take advantage of specialties and assets that might be less available during sunshine hours. Inspecting the nighttime propensities for less popular fish gives a brief look into the secret world they occupy during the peaceful hours of the evening.

5.2 Nighttime Scavenging and Regenerative Exercises

Nighttime ways of behaving reach out past simple variation to low-light circumstances; they likewise assume a vital part in rummaging and regenerative exercises. Certain fish might participate in nighttime taking care of, exploiting the accessibility of prey things that are more dynamic during the evening. Nighttime propagation, set apart by the arrival of eggs or romance presentations under the front of murkiness, grandstands the diverse manners by which less popular fish improve their ways of behaving to flourish in their surroundings.

**6. Relocation and Developments: Exploring Dynamic Scenes

6.1 Occasional Developments and Bringing forth Relocations

Movement is an enamoring part of the ways of behaving displayed by less popular freshwater fish. Occasional developments, frequently connected with generating relocations, permit fish to get to explicit environments significant for reproducing. A few animal types embrace momentous excursions, exploring waterways and feeders to arrive at their favored bringing forth grounds. The investigation of these relocation designs reveals insight into the environmental meaning of these developments and the difficulties fish face in exploring dynamic scenes.

6.2 Homing Ways of behaving and Route

The capacity of less popular fish to explore immense distances and return to explicit areas is frequently ascribed to homing ways of behaving. Whether driven by ecological signs, heavenly route, or attractive awareness, these ways of behaving feature the momentous navigational abilities of these fish. Understanding the systems behind homing ways of behaving gives important bits of knowledge into the versatile techniques that less popular fish utilize to explore the consistently changing scenes of freshwater environments.

**7. Correspondence: Quiet Discussions in the Profundities

7.1 Visual Presentations and Hue

Correspondence among less popular freshwater fish frequently includes visual presentations and dynamic hues. These visual signs serve different capabilities, from laying out strength and romance to advance notice of possible dangers. The investigation of these visual correspondence methodologies gives a window into the quiet discussions that unfurl underneath the water's surface, molding the social elements and connections of these fish.

7.2 Acoustic Signs and Vibration Correspondence

Notwithstanding visual presentations, some less popular fish take part in acoustic correspondence, utilizing sounds or vibrations to pass on data. This type of correspondence is especially significant in low-perceivability conditions or when visual signs might be deficient. Concentrating on acoustic signs and vibration correspondence upgrades how we might interpret the mind boggling manners by which less popular fish speak with one another, adding to their social designs and ways of behaving.

**8. Mental Capacities: Exploring Complex Conditions

8.1 Critical thinking and Learning

The mental capacities of less popular freshwater fish are an interesting part of their ways of behaving. A few animal categories display critical thinking abilities, adjusting to changes in their current circumstance or beating impediments. Learning ways of behaving, for example, perceiving taking care of signals or exploring through complex territories, feature the versatile insight of these fish. The investigation of mental capacities gives bits of knowledge into the manners in which less popular fish explore and flourish in their dynamic and frequently testing conditions.

8.2 Memory and Variation

Memory assumes a significant part in the ways of behaving of less popular fish, adding to their capacity to perceive natural conditions, explore complex scenes, and gain from previous encounters. Variation, both at the individual and populace levels, highlights the versatility of these fish even with ecological changes. Understanding the mental parts of their ways of behaving adds layers to the story of how less popular fish effectively explore the mind boggling snare of freshwater biological systems.

9. Connections with Different Species: Biological Elements

9.1 Hunter Prey Connections

The ways of behaving of less popular freshwater fish are unpredictably woven into the hunter prey connections that shape amphibian biological systems.

From covert hunting systems to sly moves, these ways of behaving add to the unique equilibrium between hunter and prey populaces. Concentrating on these connections gives important bits of knowledge into the natural jobs these fish play and the flowing impacts on different species inside freshwater food networks.

9.2 Mutualistic Connections and Beneficial interaction

Past hunter prey connections, less popular fish take part in mutualistic connections and beneficial interaction with different species. Cleaning ways of behaving, where certain fish go about as "cleaners" by eliminating parasites from bigger fish, epitomize the helpful procedures that add to the wellbeing of amphibian networks. Investigating these mutualistic connections reveals insight into the interconnectedness of species and the cooperative ways of behaving that shape freshwater environments.

10. Preservation Suggestions: Shielding Ways of behaving for What's in store

10.1 Dangers to Social Variety

The ways of behaving displayed by less popular freshwater fish are not invulnerable to the dangers and tensions forced by human exercises. Environment debasement, contamination, overexploitation, and environmental change can upset the normal ways of behaving of these fish, prompting decreases in populaces and modifying the mind boggling elements of freshwater biological systems. Perceiving the dangers to conduct variety is a urgent move toward forming powerful protection techniques.

10.2 Coordinating Ways of behaving into Protection Arranging

Protection endeavors pointed toward defending less popular freshwater fish should incorporate a comprehension of their ways of behaving into arranging and the executives systems. Safeguarding basic living spaces, protecting movement courses, and alleviating the effects of obtrusive species are fundamental parts of preservation arranging. Also, cultivating mindfulness about the biological significance of these ways of behaving among nearby networks and policymakers is essential for earning support for preservation drives.

4.1 Breeding Strategies and Reproductive Patterns

The freshwater environments overflow with life, and among the frequently disregarded occupants are less popular fish species displaying a spellbinding cluster of rearing methodologies and conceptive examples. These many-sided processes, molded by transformative powers and natural signs, assume a vital part in the endurance and propagation of these sea-going species. This investigation digs into the entrancing universe of rearing techniques and regenerative examples among less popular freshwater fish, revealing insight into the variety of variations and ways of behaving that add to the strength of their populaces.

**1. Presentation: The Essential Dance of Life in Freshwater Conditions

In the complex embroidery of freshwater biological systems, the domain of rearing and generation remains as a foundation of life. Less popular freshwater fish, frequently stowed away from the spotlight, take part in a heap of rearing procedures and regenerative examples that highlight their versatility to different conditions. From complex romance ceremonies to extraordinary settling ways of behaving, these species explore the difficulties of propagating their caring in the unique scenes of waterways, lakes, and streams.

**2. Occasional Rearing and Ecological Triggers

2.1 Embracing the Rhythms of Nature

Numerous less popular freshwater fish show occasional rearing examples, synchronizing their regenerative exercises with natural prompts. The evolving seasons, varieties in temperature, and adjustments in day length act as triggers for the commencement of rearing ways of behaving. These species grandstand an ability to surprise to adjust to the recurrent idea of their environments, enhancing their opportunities for conceptive accomplishment during great circumstances.

2.2 Producing Seasons and Ecological Pointers

Producing seasons among less popular fish are much of the time interspersed by unmistakable ecological pointers. Changes in water temperature, varieties in water stream, and changes in photoperiods can prompt the commencement of regenerative exercises. A few animal types might show exact timing, guaranteeing that the arrival of eggs corresponds with ideal circumstances for the endurance of posterity. The investigation of these occasional rearing examples reveals the perplexing dance of life woven into the texture of freshwater environments.

**3. Romance Shows: Nature's Expressive dance of Fascination

3.1 Elaborate Romance Customs

Romance presentations among less popular freshwater fish are charming exhibitions that go before the genuine demonstration of generating. These customs fill various needs, including mate determination, the foundation of pair bonds, and the synchronization of regenerative exercises. Elaborate balance shows, dynamic hues, and synchronized developments add to the progress of romance, guaranteeing that the ideal people meet up for effective propagation.

3.2 Tinge and Body Examples

Shading and body designs assume a pivotal part in romance showcases. Guys, specifically, frequently go through energetic variety changes or foster many-sided body examples to draw in females.

These obvious prompts signal preparation for proliferation and can show the hereditary wellness of likely mates. The investigation of romance showcases discloses the stylish and versatile parts of rearing systems among less popular freshwater fish.

**4. Settling Ways of behaving: Making Places of refuge for Posterity

4.1 Home Development and Determination

Settling ways of behaving are a sign of numerous less popular freshwater fish species, with people effectively captivating in the development of homes for the statement of eggs. Homes fluctuate broadly in structure, going from exhumed pits in the substrate to painstakingly woven structures made from plant materials. The determination of home locales is a basic part of rearing methodologies, with people picking areas that give ideal circumstances to egg improvement and sear endurance.

4.2 Fatherly and Maternal Consideration

Some less popular fish species grandstand exceptional parental consideration ways of behaving. While fatherly consideration is frequently noticed, where guys effectively watch and will more often than not eggs and broil, maternal consideration is additionally present in specific species. The division of parental obligations adds to the endurance of posterity, offering security from hunters and natural difficulties. The investigation of settling ways of behaving gives bits of knowledge into the systems utilized by these fish to guarantee the fruitful improvement of their descendants.

**5. Broadcast Generating: A Downpour of Conceptive Productivity

5.1 Mass Arrival of Gametes

Broadcast generating is a regenerative system seen in numerous less popular freshwater fish, portrayed by the mass arrival of gametes into the water segment. This system improves regenerative effectiveness, taking into account the preparation of eggs by unreservedly suspended sperm. The synchronization of generating occasions, frequently set off by natural prompts, adds to the dispersal and appropriation of posterity across the sea-going climate.

5.2 Treatment Elements

Broadcast generating presents special preparation elements, where the opportunity experience of gametes in the water section decides conceptive achievement. Factors, for example, water stream, temperature, and the planning of producing occasions impact the dispersal and destiny of treated eggs. The investigation of transmission bringing forth discloses the developmental variations that less popular freshwater fish have created to explore the difficulties of regenerative effectiveness in unique oceanic scenes.

**6. Elective Conceptive Methodologies: Adjusting to Different Conditions

6.1 Tennis shoe Guys and Satellite Producing

Some less popular freshwater fish utilize elective conceptive methodologies to upgrade their possibilities passing on their qualities. Shoe guys, for instance, embrace strategies to prepare eggs without taking part in conventional romance showcases. Satellite generating includes people taking advantage of the homes of others for their regenerative benefit. These elective procedures exhibit the adaptability and flexibility of less popular fish in different oceanic conditions.

6.2 Hermaphroditism and Sex-Changing Capacities

Hermaphroditism, where people have both male and female conceptive organs, is seen in specific less popular freshwater fish. Moreover, an animal categories display the capacity to change sex in light of natural or social variables. These special regenerative methodologies add to the flexibility of these fish populaces, empowering them to adjust to changing circumstances and enhance conceptive achievement.

**7. Challenges in Propagation: Exploring Natural Tensions

7.1 Living space Debasement and Modified Conditions

The regenerative progress of less popular freshwater fish is complicatedly connected to the wellbeing and accessibility of appropriate natural surroundings. Living space debasement, coming about because of human exercises like deforestation, urbanization, and contamination, represents a critical danger to the regenerative outcome of these fish. Adjusted conditions, remembering changes for water quality and temperature, can upset the timing and outcome of generating occasions.

7.2 Intrusive Species and Contest

The presentation of intrusive species can present difficulties to the conceptive outcome of less popular fish by changing natural elements and presenting new contenders. Intrusive species may outcompete local fish for assets or go after eggs and broil, influencing the endurance of posterity. Understanding the effects of obtrusive species on conceptive examples is pivotal for figuring out compelling protection systems.

**8. Protection Suggestions: Shielding the Dance of Life
8.1 Territory Safeguarding and Reclamation

Protection endeavors pointed toward defending the rearing techniques and regenerative examples of less popular freshwater fish should focus on natural surroundings conservation and rebuilding. Safeguarding basic generating and settling grounds, keeping up with water quality, and guaranteeing the accessibility of reasonable territories add to the progress of conceptive exercises.

Natural surroundings centered preservation drives assume a crucial part in getting the eventual fate of these fish populaces.

8.2 Alleviating Anthropogenic Dangers

Tending to anthropogenic dangers, like contamination and living space debasement, is fundamental for the protection of rearing procedures and conceptive examples. Executing and implementing guidelines to moderate the effects of human exercises on freshwater biological systems is critical. Public mindfulness and local area commitment are likewise imperative parts of preservation methodologies, cultivating a feeling of stewardship and obligation towards the insurance of these many-sided conceptive cycles.

4.2 Feeding Habits and Foraging Techniques

In the lowered domains of freshwater environments, less popular fish participate in a culinary orchestra, displaying a captivating exhibit of taking care of propensities and scrounging methods. These ways of behaving, formed by developmental transformations and natural elements, contribute not exclusively to the endurance of these sea-going species yet in addition to the biological equilibrium of their living spaces. This investigation jumps into the perplexing universe of taking care of propensities and scavenging procedures among less popular freshwater fish, uncovering the assorted systems utilized by these species to get their feasts in the unique embroidery of sea-going life.

1. Presentation: The Environmental Smorgasbord Underneath the Surface

In the oceanic embroidery, taking care of propensities and rummaging strategies of less popular freshwater fish unfurl as a spellbinding story. From the benthic voyagers filtering through dregs to the surface-staying hunters skimming bugs from the water's surface, these ways of behaving illustrate transformation and endurance in the different scenes of waterways, lakes, and streams. As we leave on this excursion, we dig into the subtleties of how these fish secure their food and add to the complicated trap of life underneath the water's surface.

2. Specialty Specialization in Taking care of: The Culinary Range of Variety

2.1 Benthic Foragers: Investigating the Profundities for Rarities

Numerous less popular freshwater fish are benthic foragers, exploring the profundities of amphibian conditions looking for food. Outfitted with particular mouths and tactile transformations, these fish filter through silt, mud, and debris to uncover spineless creatures, little scavengers, and bug hatchlings. Their taking care of propensities add to supplement cycling and assist with keeping up with the biological equilibrium of benthic environments.

2.2 Pelagic Feeders: Exploring Vast Waters for Prey

Conversely, pelagic feeders watch the untamed waters, chasing after prey things like zooplankton, little fish, or oceanic bugs. These fish are frequently furnished with smoothed out bodies and sharp detects, permitting them to proficiently explore the water section. Pelagic taking care of propensities add to the elements of untamed water environments, where the quest for prey requires vital swimming and spry moving.

**3. Channel Taking care of and Micropredation: Adjusting the Culinary Expressions

3.1 Channel Feeders: Catching Infinitesimal Culinary Enjoyments

Certain less popular fish species have sharpened the specialty of channel taking care of, removing tiny particles from the water segment. By using specific designs, for example, gill rakers or sifting device, these fish catch green growth, tiny fish, and natural debris. Channel taking care of not just grandstands the versatility of these fish to supplement rich conditions yet additionally assumes a critical part in keeping up with water lucidity and quality.

3.2 Micropredation: Hunting the Little Occupants

Micropredators among less popular freshwater fish participate in the craft of hunting little spineless creatures, bug hatchlings, or small living beings. Their scavenging procedures include key moves and accuracy to catch slippery prey. Micropredation adds to the guideline of invertebrate populaces and exhibits the different techniques these fish utilize to get their feasts in the many-sided microcosms of freshwater environments.

**4. Perusing and Brushing: The Herbivores of Freshwater Living spaces

4.1 Perusing Herbivores: Snacking on Amphibian Vegetation

Some less popular freshwater fish species embrace a herbivorous way of life, perusing on oceanic vegetation for food. Furnished with particular teeth and jaws, these herbivores assume a urgent part in forming the construction of submerged plant networks. Their taking care of propensities add to the guideline of plant development, supplement cycling, and the general soundness of freshwater territories.

4.2 Brushing Systems: Keeping up with Equilibrium in Oceanic Nurseries

Touching procedures include effectively consuming green growth and periphyton that coat lowered surfaces. Certain fish utilize their particular mouthparts to scratch or brush on surfaces like rocks, logs, or oceanic plants. Brushing propensities add to the counteraction of over the top algal development, keeping up with biological equilibrium and the stylish allure of submerged conditions.

5. Surface Taking care of: The Specialty of Skimming and Grabbing

5.1 Surface Skimmers: Exploring the Water's Skin for Prey

Surface-taking care of propensities are seen among less popular freshwater fish that skim close to the water's surface, taking advantage of the overflow of earthbound bugs or drifting prey things. These surface skimmers grandstand surprising dexterity, utilizing their specific mouths to grab bugs floating over the water. This scrounging procedure isn't just outwardly dazzling yet additionally shows the versatility of these fish to dynamic oceanic conditions.

5.2 Aeronautical Snatchers: Catching Prey from A higher place

Aeronautical snatchers are skilled at catching flying bugs or earthbound prey things from over the water's surface. Their rummaging methods include accuracy and timing as they jump from the water to grab prey in mid-air. This conduct features the flexibility of less popular fish in taking advantage of various specialties inside freshwater environments and adds to the control of bug populaces.

6. Nighttime Rummaging: Exploring the Culinary Shadows

6.1 Variations to Nighttime Life

Nighttime rummaging is a typical way of behaving among less popular freshwater fish, permitting them to take advantage of specialties and prey things that become more dynamic during the evening. Transformations to nighttime life incorporate particular tactile organs, changes in shading, and adjusted movement designs. Nighttime foragers exhibit the capacity to explore and scrounge actually in low-light circumstances.

6.2 Nighttime Taking care of Methodologies

Nighttime taking care of methodologies include effectively looking for prey in the murkiness, exploiting the expanded movement of specific creatures during the evening. Less popular fish might target nighttime spineless creatures, little fish, or even participate in primative ways of behaving under the front of haziness. Nighttime scavenging adds to the improvement of taking care of productivity and the usage of assorted food assets.

**7. Barbarian Ways of behaving: A Culinary Curve in Freshwater Biological systems

7.1 Intraspecific Predation: A System of Advantage

Inhuman ways of behaving, where people of similar species go after one another, are seen among some less popular freshwater fish. This entrepreneurial system might be set off by elements like restricted food assets, rivalry for domains, or even as a reaction to changing natural circumstances.

Human flesh consumption assumes a part in controlling populace thickness and can be a step by step process for surviving during times of shortage.

7.2 Size-Organized Savagery: Adjusting the Culinary Order

Size-organized savagery includes the predation of more modest people by bigger conspecifics. This various leveled taking care of conduct can have suggestions for populace elements, development rates, and the circulation of assets inside freshwater environments. Size-organized human flesh consumption grandstands the many-sided balance among predation and populace guideline in the culinary elements of less popular fish networks.

**8. Preservation Suggestions: Sustaining Culinary Biodiversity

8.1 Saving Basic Natural surroundings

Preservation endeavors pointed toward saving taking care of propensities and scavenging procedures of less popular freshwater fish should focus on the insurance of basic territories. Keeping up with the wellbeing and variety of submerged conditions, including benthic substrates, untamed waters, and sea-going vegetation, is fundamental for the proceeded with outcome of these culinary methodologies.

8.2 Relieving Anthropogenic Effects

Tending to anthropogenic effects like contamination, living space corruption, and overexploitation is urgent for the protection of taking care of propensities and scavenging procedures. Carrying out and upholding guidelines that relieve these effects assist with protecting the environmental equilibrium of freshwater biological systems, permitting less popular fish to proceed with their culinary jobs in keeping up with biodiversity.

4.3 Social Structures and Communication

Underneath the tranquil surface of freshwater environments, less popular fish species weave a multifaceted embroidered artwork of social designs and correspondence. While frequently eclipsed by their more prominent partners, these fish participate in nuanced connections, shaping social orders that add to the versatility and equilibrium of their oceanic networks. This investigation dives into the captivating universe of social designs and correspondence among less popular freshwater fish, revealing insight into the cooperative ways of behaving and unpredictable dialects that characterize their secret social orders.

1. **Presentation: Divulging the Public activities Underneath the Surface**

   In the fluid scenes where less popular freshwater fish flourish, social designs and correspondence assume vital parts in forming the elements of their networks.

   These fish, however frequently neglected, participate in a mind boggling dance of connections, laying out orders, framing unions, and conveying through different signs. As we set out on this excursion, we dig into the profundities of their public activities, disentangling the secrets that add to the versatility and flexibility of these amphibian social orders.

2. **Tutoring and Shoaling: The Force of Aggregate Development**
2.1 **Tutoring Elements: Security in larger groups**
Numerous less popular freshwater fish show tutoring conduct, shaping very close gatherings that move simultaneously through the water. Tutoring gives benefits like expanded insurance from hunters, upgraded searching productivity, and further developed route. The firm developments of schools exhibit the coordination and correspondence that happen among people, adding to the endurance and outcome of these fish in unique sea-going conditions.

2.2 **Shoaling Procedures: Adaptable Social Designs**
Shoaling, a less unbending type of collection contrasted with tutoring, includes fish that swim together for social reasons yet don't be guaranteed to keep up with the severe coordination saw in schools. Sandbars offer adaptability, permitting people to meet up for social collaborations while keeping a level of freedom. Understanding the elements of shoaling reveals insight into the shifted social designs displayed by less popular fish and their versatile systems in various territories.

3. **Single Propensities and Territoriality: Laying out Private Space**
3.1 **Singular Ways of life: Autonomy in the Profundities**
While tutoring and shoaling are normal social ways of behaving, some less popular freshwater fish incline toward a single way of life. These people lay out and guard domains, guaranteeing admittance to assets like food, asylum, and possible mates. The investigation of single propensities gives bits of knowledge into the elements impacting territoriality and the manners by which people streamline their lone presence in assorted amphibian conditions.

3.2 **Territoriality and Progressive systems: Keeping Everything under control in Social orders**
Regional way of behaving frequently prompts the foundation

of progressive systems inside fish social orders. Prevailing people guard prime domains, while subordinate fish might involve less helpful regions. These orders impact admittance to assets and open doors for proliferation. Looking at the elements of territoriality reveals the social designs that arise inside less popular fish populaces, displaying the harmony among contest and participation.

4. **Agreeable Systems: Strength in Coordinated effort**

   4.1 Gathering Scavenging: Agreeable Taking care of Ways of behaving

   Agreeable systems among less popular freshwater fish stretch out past basic gathering. A few animal varieties participate in helpful scrounging, where people cooperate to find and catch prey. This cooperative conduct improves taking care of productivity and asset procurement. Investigating helpful scavenging reveals insight into the mind boggling manners by which fish impart and organize their activities for common advantage.

   4.2 Synchronized Generating: Aggregate Regenerative Endeavors

   Synchronized generating is a noteworthy helpful methodology seen in specific less popular fish species. People coordinate their conceptive exercises, delivering eggs and sperm all the while. This synchronized methodology improves the probability of effective preparation and upgrades the endurance of posterity. Understanding the systems behind synchronized generating gives experiences into the correspondence signals that trigger aggregate regenerative endeavors.

5. **Correspondence: The Quiet Language Beneath the Surface**

   5.1 Visual Presentations and Shading: Flagging Aims

   Correspondence among less popular freshwater fish frequently includes visual presentations and dynamic hues. These visual signs serve different capabilities, from laying out strength and romance to advance notice of likely dangers. The investigation of these visual correspondence methodologies gives a window into the quiet discussions that unfurl beneath the water's surface, molding the social elements and cooperations of these fish.

5.2 Acoustic Signs and Vibration Correspondence: Past Obvious Signals

Notwithstanding visual showcases, some less popular fish participate in acoustic correspondence, utilizing sounds or vibrations to pass on data. This type of correspondence is especially significant in low-perceivability conditions or when visual signs might be lacking. Concentrating on acoustic signs and vibration correspondence upgrades how we might interpret the unpredictable manners by which less popular fish speak with one another, adding to their social designs and ways of behaving.

6. Mental Capacities: Exploring Complex Social Conditions

6.1 Critical thinking and Learning: Versatile Knowledge

The mental capacities of less popular freshwater fish are a captivating part of their social ways of behaving. A few animal varieties show critical thinking abilities, adjusting to changes in their current circumstance or beating deterrents. Learning ways of behaving, for example, perceiving meaningful gestures or exploring through complex social scenes, exhibit the versatile insight of these fish.

The investigation of mental capacities gives experiences into the manners in which less popular fish explore and flourish in their dynamic and frequently testing social conditions.

6.2 Memory and Social Transformation: The Job of Involvement

Memory assumes a critical part in the social ways of behaving of less popular fish, adding to their capacity to perceive recognizable people, explore social pecking orders, and gain from previous encounters. Social variation, both at the individual and populace levels, highlights the strength of these fish even with social changes. Understanding the mental parts of their ways of behaving adds layers to the story of how less popular fish effectively explore the mind boggling social trap of freshwater environments.

7. **Cooperations with Different Species: Biological Elements**

   7.1 Hunter Prey Cooperations: Molding Environment Equilibrium

   The ways of behaving of less popular freshwater fish are complicatedly woven into the hunter prey connections that shape oceanic biological systems. From secretive hunting systems to hesitant moves, these ways of behaving add to the unique harmony between hunter and prey populaces. Concentrating on these associations gives important bits of knowledge into the natural jobs these fish play and the flowing consequences for different species inside freshwater food networks.

   7.2 Mutualistic Connections and Advantageous interaction: Cooperative Environment Administrations

   Past hunter prey communications, less popular fish participate in mutualistic connections and advantageous interaction with different species. Cleaning ways of behaving, where certain fish go about as "cleaners" by eliminating parasites from bigger fish, embody the agreeable systems that add to the wellbeing of amphibian networks. Investigating these mutualistic connections reveals insight into the interconnectedness of species and the cooperative ways of behaving that shape freshwater biological systems.

8. **Protection Suggestions: Shielding Social Elements**

   8.1 Safeguarding Basic Environments and Relocation Courses

   Preservation endeavors pointed toward shielding the social designs and correspondence of less popular freshwater fish should focus on the assurance of basic environments and relocation courses. Saving the different conditions where fish structure schools, lay out regions, and take part in friendly collaborations is fundamental for keeping up with the biological equilibrium of freshwater environments.

8.2 Alleviating Anthropogenic Dangers

Tending to anthropogenic dangers, like contamination, living space debasement, and overfishing, is urgent for the protection of social designs and correspondence among less popular fish. Executing and upholding guidelines to moderate these effects assist with shielding the complicated cultural elements that add to the flexibility and versatility of freshwater fish populaces.

Chapter 5

The Aquarium Enthusiast's Guide

1 Leaving on an Excursion into Oceanic Magnificence

The universe of aquariums is a dazzling domain where lovers can bring a cut of sea-going life into their homes. Whether you're a carefully prepared specialist or a newbie to the universe of aquariums, this extensive aide intends to be your friend on an excursion through the miracles of oceanic domains. From choosing the right tank to making a flourishing environment and really focusing on a different exhibit of fish and plants, this guide offers experiences, tips, and motivation for aquarium devotees, everything being equal.

2. Picking the Right Aquarium: Establishments for Progress

2.1 Tank Size and Arrangement: Setting the Stage

Choosing the right aquarium is the main significant stage on your sea-going excursion. Think about elements like accessible space, spending plan, and your degree of responsibility. Whether you choose a little work area tank or a huge exhibit aquarium, the size and position of your tank assume a critical part in the outcome of your oceanic endeavor.

2.2 Glass versus Acrylic: Gauging the Choices

The decision among glass and acrylic aquariums includes contemplations of toughness, clearness, and weight. Understanding the attributes of every material assists you with settling on an educated choice in view of your inclinations and the particular necessities of the amphibian climate you mean to make.

2.3 Freshwater versus Saltwater: Plunging into Environment Variety

Choosing a freshwater and a saltwater aquarium is a key decision that impacts the kind of fish and plants you can keep. Every choice has its special difficulties and prizes. Freshwater aquariums are frequently suggested for fledglings, while saltwater arrangements offer a dazzling exhibit of marine life yet require extra mastery.

3. Fundamental Hardware: Building the Establishment for Progress

3.1 Filtration Frameworks: Establishing a Spotless and Clear Climate

Compelling filtration is vital for keeping a solid aquarium. Investigate the different kinds of filtration frameworks, from mechanical to organic and synthetic, and comprehend how they add to water lucidity, compound equilibrium, and the general prosperity of your amphibian occupants.

3.2 Lighting: Enlightening the Submerged Scene

Picking the right lighting for your aquarium is in excess of a question of style. Light assumes a pivotal part in the development of plants and the prosperity of fish. Investigate the various kinds of aquarium lighting, including Drove, fluorescent, and metal halide choices, and figure out how to make the best lighting conditions for your oceanic environment.

3.3 Warming and Temperature Control: Guaranteeing Agreeable Conditions

Keeping a steady temperature is fundamental for the wellbeing and essentialness of your aquarium's occupants. Find out about aquarium radiators, thermometers, and temperature regulators to establish an agreeable and predictable climate for your fish and plants.

4. Aquascaping: Planning a Stunning Submerged Scene

4.1 Substrate Determination: Making the Establishment

The decision of substrate makes way for your aquarium's tasteful and utilitarian angles. Investigate choices like rock, sand, and established substrates, taking into account the necessities of your picked plants and the visual effect you need to accomplish.

4.2 Rocks and Driftwood: Adding Normal Components

Rocks and driftwood not just upgrade the visual allure of your aquarium yet additionally give concealing spots and haven to fish. Comprehend how to choose and organize these components to make a naturalistic and agreeable submerged scene.

4.3 Plants: Implanting Life and Oxygen

Live plants carry a dynamic and regular component to your aquarium. Dive into the universe of oceanic plants, from simple to-really focus on assortments to those that require more specific consideration. Find out about establishing methods, substrates for plant development, and the advantages of an established aquarium.

5. Choosing Fish: Building a Different and Amicable People group

5.1 Investigating Fish Species: Addressing the Necessities of Your Tank

Prior to acquainting fish with your aquarium, exhaustive examination is fundamental. Investigate the qualities, ways of behaving, and similarity of various fish species. Consider factors like size, demeanor, and water boundaries to make an agreeable and flourishing local area.

5.2 Local area versus Species-Just Tanks: Adjusting Biodiversity

Pick between a local area tank, which houses various viable species, and an animal groups just tank, which centers around a solitary sort of fish.

Every choice has its benefits, and understanding the elements of the two assists you with making an aquarium that lines up with your inclinations and objectives.

5.3 Presenting Fish: Adjusting and Observing

The most common way of acquainting fish with your aquarium requires cautious acclimation to forestall pressure and guarantee a smooth progress. Become familiar with the means for adapting fish and observing their way of behaving to recognize indications of trouble. Understanding the complexities of fish acquaintance contributes with the general prosperity of your sea-going local area.

6. Routine Support: Supporting a Solid Biological system

6.1 Water Changes: Keeping up with Water Quality

Customary water changes are a foundation of aquarium support. Investigate the recurrence and techniques for water changes, understanding how they add to water quality, supplement balance, and the general soundness of your aquarium occupants.

6.2 Cleaning and Green growth Control: Finding Some kind of harmony

Keeping a spotless aquarium includes overseeing green growth development and eliminating garbage. Investigate procedures for green growth control, substrate cleaning, and keeping up with gear to establish an outwardly engaging and solid climate.

6.3 Testing Water Boundaries: Guaranteeing Ideal Circumstances

Standard testing of water boundaries is fundamental for checking the wellbeing of your aquarium. Find out about the significance of testing for boundaries like pH, smelling salts, nitrites, and nitrates, and comprehend how to decipher test results to make informed changes in accordance with your aquarium's current circumstance.

7. High level Themes: Digging Further into Aquarium Ability

7.1 Reproducing: Sustaining New Life

For lovers hoping to extend their aquarium side interest, rearing fish adds another component of fervor. Investigate the essentials of fish rearing, including choosing reproducing matches, giving the right circumstances, and really focusing on fry as they create.

7.2 Aquascaping Styles: Making Creative Magnum opuses

Aquascaping is a work of art that permits aquarium devotees to communicate innovativeness and plan abilities. Find different aquascaping styles, from nature aquariums to Dutch and iwagumi designs, and learn methods for making outwardly shocking submerged scenes.

7.3 High level Fishkeeping Methods: Difficulties and Prizes

Progressed fishkeeping strategies, for example, keeping up with specialty tanks or rearing interesting species, give a remunerating challenge to experienced fans. Dive into subjects, for example, specialty rearing ventures, biotope aquariums, and establishing conditions for explicit kinds of fish.

8. Investigating Normal Issues: Conquering Difficulties

8.1 Illness Anticipation and Treatment: Really focusing on Feeble Fish

Perceiving indications of ailment and executing sickness avoidance measures are critical parts of aquarium care. Investigate normal fish sicknesses, their causes, and therapy choices to keep a sound and illness free aquarium.

8.2 Managing Green growth: Systems for Control

Green growth can be a tireless test in aquariums, influencing feel and water quality. Find out about the various kinds of green growth, their causes, and compelling methodologies for forestalling and controlling green growth development.

8.3 Resolving Social Issues: Figuring out Fish Conduct

Fish conduct can give significant experiences into the wellbeing and prosperity of your aquarium's occupants. Investigate normal social issues, like hostility, stowing away, or surprising swimming examples, and comprehend how to resolve these issues to establish an agreeable climate.

9. Protection and Moral Contemplations: Dependable Aquarium Keeping

9.1 Moral Obtaining: Supporting Feasible Practices

Capable aquarium keeping includes moral obtaining of fish and plants. Find out about the significance of supporting reasonable works on, picking hostage reproduced examples, and staying away from species that are compromised or gathered unreasonably from nature.

9.2 Protection Drives: Adding to Oceanic Biodiversity

Aquarium devotees can assume a part in oceanic protection. Investigate drives and practices that add to the safeguarding of oceanic biodiversity, living space protection, and the prosperity of fish in nature.

5.1 Lesser-Known Fish Suitable for Home Aquariums

Aquarium devotees frequently look for extraordinary and less popular fish species to differentiate their sea-going scenes. While famous species like bettas and tetras rule the side interest, there's a mother lode of less popular fish that can add interest, variety, and appeal to your home aquarium.

In this investigation, we dive into the entrancing universe of less popular fish that are reasonable for home aquariums as well as bring a hint of curiosity and uniqueness to your submerged safe house.

1. **The Heavenly Pearl Danio (Danio margaritatus): A Gem in Smaller than normal**
   The Heavenly Pearl Danio, otherwise called the System Rasbora, is a little yet dazzling fish that hails from Southeast Asia. This scaled down jewel flaunts a hitting appearance with radiant blue and orange tones suggestive of a brilliant night sky. Obviously appropriate for nano aquariums, these tranquil fish flourish in all around established arrangements with delicate water stream. Their little size and quiet attitude make them astounding allies for other non-forceful species in local area tanks.

2. **The Glass Catfish (Kryptopterus vitreolus): Straightforward Polish**
   In the event that you're searching for a fish with a remarkable turn, the Glass Catfish is a dazzling decision. Local to Southeast

Asia, this straightforward species permits an unmistakable perspective on its interior organs, making an entrancing and ethereal impact. While they value the organization of their own sort, Glass Catfish coincide calmly with other non-forceful tankmates. Furnish them with curbed lighting and adequate concealing spaces to reproduce the peacefulness of their regular territories.

3. **The Elephantnose Fish (Gnathonemus petersii): A Captivating Electric Touch**

   For fans looking for a fish with an unmistakable appearance and conduct, the Elephantnose Fish is a noteworthy choice. Starting from West and Focal Africa, these fish are perceived for their stretched noses and electroreceptive capacities. The Elephantnose Fish explores its environmental factors utilizing feeble electric fields, adding an interesting aspect to your aquarium. Keep them in gatherings to lighten pressure, and give a delicate substrate and concealing spots to imitate their normal territory.

4. **The Peacock Gudgeon (Tateurndina ocellicauda): A Sprinkle of Variety**

   With its lively tints and striking examples, the Peacock Gudgeon is a bright expansion to freshwater aquariums. Local to Papua New Guinea, this little and quiet species includes an enamoring show of orange, blue, and green. Ideal for established tanks with delicate water stream, Peacock Gudgeons flourish in conditions that recreate their local streams. They are reasonable for local area arrangements, particularly when matched with non-forceful tankmates.

5. **The Bristlenose Catfish (Ancistrus sp.): Nature's Green growth Eater**

   For aquarium devotees looking for a proficient green growth eater with a one of a kind appearance, the Bristlenose Catfish is a fantastic decision.

   This shielded catfish, known for its unmistakable fiber like designs all over, assumes an important part in keeping a perfect tank by consuming green growth. Hailing from South America, Bristlenose Catfish are strong, versatile, and appropriate for local area aquariums. Their charming facial highlights and green growth clearing capacities make them a #1 among aquarists.

6. **The Red Badis (dario): A Gem in Small scale**
Another smaller than normal wonder, the Red Badis, is a little fish that sneaks up all of a sudden of variety. Local to India, these energetic fish feature shades of red, blue, and green, making them an enamoring expansion to nano aquariums. Regardless of their little size, Red Badis can be regional, particularly during the reproducing season. Give adequate concealing spaces and consider an animal groups just arrangement or select tankmates cautiously to guarantee an amicable climate.

7. **The Pencilfish (Nannostomus sp.): Polish in Effortlessness**
With their slim bodies and tranquil nature, Pencilfish carry a dash of polish to home aquariums. Starting from South America, different types of Pencilfish are accessible in the aquarium exchange. These shoaling fish flourish in gatherings and favor very much established tanks with curbed lighting. Known for their unmistakable pencil-like shape and stifled colors, they add effortlessness and appeal to local area aquariums without the regional propensities found in a few different animal categories.

8. **The Halfbeak (Dermogenys spp.): Outlandish Surface Occupants**
For aquarium devotees looking for fish that possess different water levels, the Halfbeak is an exceptional decision. These surface-abiding fish, named for their particular extended lower jaws, add an extraordinary touch to aquariums. Beginning from Southeast Asia, Halfbeaks value roomy tanks with open swimming regions. Their particular shape and conduct make them a fascinating point of convergence, particularly in aquariums with quiet, mid-level swimmers.

9. **The Kuhli Loach (Pangio kuhlii): Unpretentious Polish in Substrate**

   Known for their eel-like appearance and quiet disposition, Kuhli Loaches carry unobtrusive class to the substrate of home aquariums. Local to Southeast Asia, these nighttime fish value concealing spaces, making them ideal for established tanks with delicate substrates. Kuhli Loaches are social animals, so think about keeping them in gatherings to empower normal ways of behaving and diminish pressure. Their remarkable appearance and interesting conduct make them a magnificent expansion to local area arrangements.

10. **The Brilliant Miracle Killifish (Aplocheilus lineatus): A Sprinkle of Distinctiveness**

    Assuming you're looking for a fish that consolidates lively tones with a functioning character, the Brilliant Miracle Killifish possesses all the necessary qualities. Local to India and Sri Lanka, this species is perceived for its striking brilliant yellow body and dynamic swimming way of behaving. While it tends to be kept in local area arrangements, guarantee that tankmates are non-forceful and will not outcompete the Brilliant Marvel Killifish during taking care of. Give more than adequate swimming space and concealing spots to take care of their dynamic nature.

11. **The Freshwater Pipefish (Microphis deocata): Submerged Polish**

    For those fascinated by the family members of seahorses, the Freshwater Pipefish offers an exceptional and enthralling choice. Beginning from India, these thin fish have extended bodies and offer likenesses with seahorses concerning appearance and care. Remember that Freshwater Pipefish are more difficult to really focus on than a few different animal varieties, requiring specific eating regimens and thoughtfulness regarding water boundaries. A deeply grounded and painstakingly kept up with aquarium is fundamental for their prosperity.

12. **The Ricefish (Oryzias spp.): Fragile Excellence**
Ricefish, hailing from Asia, are a gathering of little and fragile species that add magnificence to home aquariums. With their straightforward balances and inconspicuous tones, they make an ethereal and quiet environment. Ricefish are appropriate for planted aquariums with delicate water stream. Given their little size, they can be kept in gatherings, adding to a feeling of regular concordance in the tank.

5.2 Tank Setup and Environmental Requirements
Setting up an even and proper climate is fundamental while bringing less popular fish species into your aquarium. The progress of keeping these unlikely treasures lies in repeating their normal natural surroundings as intently as could really be expected. In this investigation, we dive into the complexities of tank arrangement and natural necessities, uncovering the key components that add to the wellbeing, prosperity, and dynamic quality of less popular fish in the home aquarium.

**1. Investigating Species-Explicit Requirements: The Establishment for Progress
Prior to leaving on the arrangement of your aquarium, careful examination into the particular requirements of the picked less popular fish species is essential. Each fish has extraordinary necessities with respect to water boundaries, temperature, pH levels, and tank size. Understanding the normal territory of the species helps in establishing a reasonable climate, lessening pressure, and advancing regular ways of behaving.

2. Tank Size and Aspects: Giving Satisfactory Room
The size of the aquarium assumes a urgent part in the prosperity of the occupants. Consider the grown-up size and swimming propensities for the picked species while deciding the proper tank size. For more modest fish like the Heavenly Pearl Danio, a nano or little aquarium might get the job done, while bigger species like the Elephantnose Fish require more open facilities. Sufficient

swimming space guarantees that fish can show their normal ways of behaving and domains.

3. Filtration Frameworks: Keeping up with Water Quality

Successful filtration is fundamental for keeping up with ideal water quality in the aquarium. Less popular fish, similar to some other species, flourish in perfect and very much oxygenated water. Pick a filtration framework that suits the size of the tank and think about the particular necessities of the fish. A few animal types might favor delicate water stream, while others, similar to the Glass Catfish, may require a more quelled ebb and flow to flourish.

4. Substrate Choice: Mirroring Regular habitats

Choosing the right substrate is a vital part of repeating the regular habitat of less popular fish. For species like the Peacock Gudgeon that appreciate filtering through the substrate, a fine sand or rock substrate is great. Then again, base dwelling fish like Kuhli Loaches benefit from delicate substrates that imitate the riverbeds or sloppy bottoms of their local territories.

5. Aquascaping: Making Concealing Spots and Regions

Aquascaping goes past feel; it assumes a huge part in the prosperity of less popular fish. Imitating the normal natural surroundings includes giving concealing spots, caverns, and designs that take care of the particular requirements of the picked species. Think about the inclinations of the fish; for example, the Elephantnose Fish values concealing spots, while the Red Badis might require thickly established regions for domains.

6. Lighting: Adjusting Style and Fish Conduct

Proper lighting adds to both the visual allure of the aquarium and the prosperity of the fish. Research the lighting inclinations of the picked species; some might favor stifled lighting, while others, as live plants, may require more splendid circumstances. Make a lighting plan that mirrors normal day-night cycles to advance regular ways of behaving and lessen pressure.

7. Water Boundaries: Keeping up with Dependability

Water boundaries are basic for the wellbeing and endurance of less popular fish. Research the ideal temperature, pH levels, and water hardness for the particular species you expect to keep. Use solid water testing units to screen these boundaries routinely and make changes on a case by case basis. Stable water conditions are fundamental for diminishing pressure and advancing normal ways of behaving among your fish.

8. Warming and Temperature Control: Guaranteeing Agreeable Circumstances

Keeping a steady and reasonable temperature is vital for the general prosperity of less popular fish. Introduce a quality aquarium warmer and thermometer to manage and screen water temperature. Various species might have explicit temperature inclinations, so tailor the circumstances to match the regular natural surroundings of the fish. Giving a reliable temperature forestalls pressure and supports fundamental natural cycles.

9. Stylistic layout and Tank Embellishments: Upgrading Feel and Usefulness

Integrating stylistic layout and tank extras not just upgrades the visual allure of the aquarium yet additionally fills practical needs for the fish. Use plants, rocks, driftwood, and different beautifications that mirror the regular habitat of the picked species. Guarantee that stylistic layout gives reasonable concealing spots and regions, adding to the general solace and security of the fish.

10. Oxygenation: Guaranteeing Satisfactory Oxygen Levels

Appropriate oxygenation is imperative for the soundness of less popular fish, particularly in thickly loaded aquariums. Pick a reasonable pneumatic machine and air stones to upgrade oxygen trade at the water's surface. Satisfactory air circulation is especially significant in arrangements with bigger or more dynamic species that might have higher oxygen prerequisites.

11. Tankmates: Picking Viable Partners

While choosing tankmates for less popular fish, similarity is vital. Research the social ways of behaving, demeanors, and size contrasts between species to forestall hostility and regional debates. A few animal categories flourish in local area arrangements, while others, similar to the Red Badis, may favor species-just tanks to limit pressure and contest.

12. Quarantine Strategies: Forestalling Infection Spread

Prior to bringing less popular fish into the fundamental aquarium, carry out a quarantine technique. This preparatory step forestalls the spread of infections and parasites.

Quarantine tanks ought to duplicate the primary tank conditions, taking into account perception and expected treatment of fresh debuts before they join the laid out local area.

13. Upkeep Schedule: Supporting a Sound Environment

Laying out an ordinary upkeep routine is vital for supporting a sound aquarium climate. Perform routine water changes to keep up with water quality, clean channels, and screen gear consistently. Noticing fish conduct and appearance during upkeep gives important bits of knowledge into their general prosperity.

14. Checking and Changing: Adjusting to Changing Requirements

Consistently screen the way of behaving, wellbeing, and generally speaking state of the less popular fish in your aquarium. Be mindful of any indications of stress, sickness, or changes in conduct. Change natural circumstances depending on the situation, taking into account factors like occasional changes, rearing ways of behaving, or the expansion of new tankmates.

5.3 Tips for Breeding and Caring for Hidden Treasures

Rearing and really focusing on less popular fish species in the home aquarium is a fulfilling and complicated venture. Whether you're enraptured by the lively shades of the Divine Pearl Danio or the novel ways of behaving of the Elephantnose Fish, fruitful rearing requires a profound comprehension of the particular necessities, ways of behaving, and conceptive methodologies of every species. In this far reaching guide, we investigate a scope of tips and contemplations to assist you with exploring the thrilling universe of rearing and really focusing on these secret fortunes.

1. **Top to bottom Species Exploration: Know Your Unexpected, yet invaluable treasures**
   Prior to setting out on a reproducing project, dig into itemized research on the particular species you mean to raise. Grasping the regular natural surroundings, ways of behaving, and regenerative procedures of the picked fish is key. Every species has extraordinary necessities, like favored water boundaries, dietary requirements, and rearing circumstances. Know about the social elements, similarity, and a particular triggers for reproducing conduct.

2. **Make Ideal Reproducing Conditions: Emulating Nature**
   Reproducing the common habitat of the picked species is fundamental to initiate rearing ways of behaving. Change tank boundaries, including temperature, pH, and water hardness, to line up with the states of their local natural surroundings.

   A few animal groups might require explicit substrates for egg-laying or explicit water stream conditions for effective multiplication. Establishing a climate that intently impersonates their regular setting lessens pressure and supports normal reproducing ways of behaving.

3. **Select Solid Reproducing Stock: Quality Matters**
   Picking solid and strong rearing stock is vital for effective proliferation. Select people that show energetic varieties, solid body construction, and dynamic ways of behaving. Stay away from fish with indications of sickness, deformations, or irregularities. Solid reproducing stock adds to the general progress of the rearing task and guarantees the prosperity of the posterity.

4. **Give Reasonable Concealing Spots: Making Places of refuge**
   Many fish species, particularly those considered less popular, display explicit rearing ways of behaving that include tracking down secure areas for laying eggs or safeguarding fry. Consolidate appropriate concealing spots, like caverns, plants, or complex embellishments, to give places of refuge to rearing matches and their posterity. These concealing spots imitate the regular haven choices in their local environments, cultivating a conviction that all is good.

5. **Temperature Control: Setting off Reproducing Seasons**
   For specific species, controlling the temperature can go about as a trigger for reproducing ways of behaving. Research the occasional examples of your picked fish in the wild and change the aquarium temperature likewise. Imitating the changing seasons can prompt rearing circumstances, animating romance ways of behaving and regenerative exercises.

6. **Carry out a Detachment Procedure: Safeguarding Fry**
   Whenever reproducing has happened, it's vital for carry out a detachment methodology to safeguard the fry from possible predation by grown-up fish. Reproducing traps, separate rearing tanks, or the essential utilization of dividers can keep grown-ups from consuming or pestering the weak fry. This detachment likewise considers centered care and observing of the fry's development and improvement.

7. **Legitimate Sustenance: Supporting Development and Wellbeing**
   Giving a decent and nutritious eating regimen is urgent for the wellbeing and improvement of both reproducing grown-ups and their posterity. Research the dietary inclinations of the picked species, and proposition a fluctuated diet that incorporates excellent pieces, pellets, live or frozen food sources, and, if pertinent, specific fry food. Legitimate sustenance upholds ideal development, hue, and conceptive wellbeing.

8. **Water Quality Upkeep: A Key to Progress**

    Keeping up with perfect water quality is basic for the outcome of any rearing venture. Customary water changes, effective filtration, and cautious observing of water boundaries add to a sound and stable climate. Recently brought forth fry are many times more delicate to changes in water conditions, accentuating the requirement for fastidious water quality administration.

9. **Notice and Record Ways of behaving: Figuring out Reproducing Cycles**

    Persevering perception of fish ways of behaving is an important device for grasping rearing cycles and perceiving indications of romance, mating, or likely issues. Keep definite records of ways of behaving, like changes in tinge, romance ceremonies, and egg-laying exercises. This documentation supports foreseeing reproducing cycles, distinguishing fruitful coordinates, and changing consideration methodologies likewise.

10. **Persistence and Perception: Keys to Progress**

    Reproducing and really focusing on less popular fish require tolerance and a sharp eye for perception. Fruitful rearing ventures might take time, particularly assuming that the picked species has explicit reproducing conditions or ways of behaving. Be patient and permit normal ways of behaving to unfurl. Customary perception gives bits of knowledge into the advancement of reproducing matches and the prosperity of the posterity.

11. **Tending to Hostility and Similarity: Keeping up with Agreement**

    In people group arrangements, overseeing hostility and guaranteeing similarity among rearing matches and tankmates is fundamental. A few animal types might become regional or forceful during the rearing season. Screen fish communications intently and be ready to isolate people on the off chance that animosity becomes dangerous. Picking viable tankmates and giving more than adequate concealing spots can assist with keeping up with amicability in the aquarium.

12. **Quarantine New Augmentations: Forestalling Sickness Spread**

   While acquainting new fish with a rearing arrangement, execute a quarantine convention to forestall the spread of infections. Quarantine tanks take into consideration perception and expected treatment of new increases before they join the rearing local area. Sickness anticipation is basic, particularly during delicate periods like reproducing, as stress can make fish more powerless to ailments.

13. **Research Parental Consideration Ways of behaving: Sustaining Posterity**

   For species that display parental consideration ways of behaving, understanding the job of each parent in focusing on the posterity is vital. A few animal varieties monitor eggs or broil steadily, while others may just have one parent engaged with care.

   Exploring these ways of behaving assists aquarists with expecting the degree of care required and whether any mediations, for example, eliminating eggs or sear, are important.

14. **Plan for Fry Development and Dispersion: Reasonable Practices**

   As fry develop, think about an arrangement for their circulation or rehoming. Congestion can prompt pressure, contest for assets, and expected hostility. Supportable reproducing rehearses include making arrangements for the development of the fry and finding reasonable homes for them, whether through reception by different specialists, exchange with nearby fish stores, or laying out discrete local area tanks.

15. **Record Rearing Achievement and Difficulties: Learning and Getting to the next level**

Keep up with nitty gritty records of rearing triumphs and difficulties. Archiving each rearing venture gives important experiences into the ways of behaving, conditions, and factors that add to progress or challenges. Gain from each insight, adjust care procedures as needs be, and apply freshly discovered information to future reproducing attempts.

Chapter 6

Conservation Efforts

1 The Basic of Freshwater Fish Preservation

Freshwater fish, frequently eclipsed by their marine partners, assume a significant part in the fragile equilibrium of sea-going environments. These less popular species, with their one of a kind transformations and ways of behaving, are confronting expanding dangers following environment obliteration, contamination, environmental change, and overexploitation. Preservation endeavors for freshwater fish are fundamental for saving biodiversity as well as for keeping up with the strength of freshwater environments and getting assets for human populaces. In this extensive investigation, we dig into the diverse universe of freshwater fish preservation, analyzing the difficulties, drives, and the essential job of aggregate activity.

2. The Territory of Freshwater Fish Biodiversity: A Dubious Equilibrium

2.1. Dangers to Freshwater Fish Biodiversity

Freshwater fish face a variety of dangers that endanger their reality. Territory obliteration, essentially determined by urbanization, rural development, and dam development, changes the regular progression of waterways and upsets basic rearing and taking care of grounds. Contamination from horticultural overflow, modern releases, and untreated sewage represents a critical danger to water quality, influencing fish wellbeing and generation. Environmental change further fuels these difficulties, prompting shifts in temperature, adjusted precipitation examples, and territory misfortune.

2.2. Overexploitation and Impractical Fishing Practices

Overfishing, driven by the interest for food and the aquarium exchange, represents an extreme danger to numerous freshwater fish species. Unreasonable fishing works on, including the utilization of horrendous stuff and the catch of adolescents, add to populace declines. Moreover, the presentation of non-local species for hydroponics or sporting fishing can prompt rivalry, predation, and the spread of sicknesses, further compromising local fish populaces.

3. Preservation Drives: A Worldwide Undertaking

3.1. Laying out Safeguarded Regions and Stores

One vital technique in freshwater fish preservation is the foundation of safeguarded regions and stores.

These regions give asylum to fish populaces, permitting them to repeat, feed, and keep up with normal ways of behaving without the prompt danger of natural surroundings annihilation or overfishing. Planning and dealing with these stores require joint effort between legislatures, preservation associations, and neighborhood networks.

3.2. Living space Rebuilding and Network

Endeavors to reestablish debased territories and further develop network inside freshwater biological systems are key to protection achievement. Reestablishing riparian zones, eliminating boundaries like dams, and executing manageable land-use rehearses add to the general strength of freshwater living spaces. Reestablished availability permits fish to move, generate, and access assorted territories critical for their life cycles.

3.3. Maintainable Fisheries The board

Executing supportable fisheries the board rehearses is fundamental for offsetting human necessities with the protection of freshwater fish.

This incorporates laying out get limits, controlling stuff types, and upholding occasional terminations to safeguard producing grounds. Local area based administration, where neighborhood networks are effectively engaged with navigation, has demonstrated successful in guaranteeing the drawn out supportability of fisheries.

3.4. Intrusive Species Control

Controlling and overseeing intrusive species is basic to protecting local freshwater fish populaces. Intrusive species can outcompete local species for assets, present infections, and disturb natural equilibrium. Annihilation or control programs, frequently including the evacuation of intrusive species and territory reclamation, are executed to moderate their effect on local biodiversity.

3.5. Examination and Observing

Continuous exploration and observing endeavors are basic to understanding the situation with freshwater fish populaces, distinguishing dangers, and assessing the viability of preservation measures. Cooperative drives between researchers, protection associations, and nearby networks add to a far reaching comprehension of the complicated elements inside freshwater environments.

4. Contextual analyses: Preservation Examples of overcoming adversity

4.1. The Renewed introduction of the European Sturgeon

The European sturgeon, when near the precarious edge of elimination due to overfishing and living space corruption, has seen a wonderful circle back through designated preservation endeavors.

Renewed introduction programs, territory reclamation, and severe fishing guidelines have added to the recuperation of this famous species. The progress of the European sturgeon protection fills in as a demonstration of the positive results reachable through coordinated activity.

4.2. The Protection of Mekong Monster Catfish

The Mekong Monster Catfish, one of the world's biggest freshwater fish, confronted an unsafe downfall because of dam development, overfishing, and natural surroundings corruption. Preservation drives in the Mekong Stream bowl, remembering the foundation of safeguarded regions and guidelines for fishing rehearses, have prompted the adjustment of the Mekong Goliath Catfish populace. The continuous endeavors underline the significance of local participation in tending to transboundary protection challenges.

5. Local area Contribution: A Mainstay of Protection

5.1. Enabling Neighborhood People group

The association of neighborhood networks is indispensable to the outcome of freshwater fish preservation. Enabling people group to effectively partake in navigation, the executives, and checking cultivates a feeling of stewardship and obligation. Cooperative endeavors that consolidate customary information and practices frequently lead to more economical and socially delicate protection results.

5.2. Manageable Jobs and Options

Tending to the financial parts of protection is pivotal for making long haul progress. Drives that give elective vocations to networks reliant upon impractical fishing rehearses, like hydroponics, ecotourism, or supportable horticulture, add to both protection objectives and the prosperity of nearby populaces.

6. Difficulties and Future Headings

6.1. Environmental Change Effects

The speeding up effects of environmental change represent extra difficulties to freshwater fish protection. Climbing temperatures, modified precipitation examples, and outrageous climate occasions can upset the biological equilibrium of freshwater environments. Versatile techniques, including the production of environment strong territories and the ID of environment brilliant protection rehearses, are basic.

6.2. Political Will and Worldwide Participation

The outcome of freshwater fish preservation depends on political will and worldwide participation. Facilitated endeavors among countries, upheld by peaceful accords and settlements, are crucial for address transboundary protection challenges.

Promotion for the consideration of freshwater biological systems in worldwide preservation plans guarantees that these essential natural surroundings get the consideration and security they merit.

6.3. Public Mindfulness and Schooling

Raising public mindfulness about the significance of freshwater fish and the difficulties they face is basic for gathering support for protection endeavors. Instructive projects, outreach drives, and organizations with schools and neighborhood networks add to building a voting demographic for freshwater fish preservation. Drawing in general society in resident science projects likewise encourages a feeling of association with freshwater biological systems.

6.1 Endangered Lesser-Known Freshwater Fish

The variety of freshwater biological systems harbors a bunch of less popular fish species, each assuming a one of a kind part in the sensitive equilibrium of sea-going life. Sadly, large numbers of these unexpected, yet invaluable treasures are wavering near the precarious edge of eradication because of a variety of dangers going from territory obliteration to overfishing. In this investigation, we jump into the situation of imperiled less popular freshwater fish, revealing insight into their significance, the difficulties they face, and the basic for protection endeavors to guarantee their endurance.

1. **The Basic Status of Jeopardized Less popular Freshwater Fish**

   1.1. The Neglected Species

   While magnetic megafauna frequently capture everyone's attention in protection conversations, less popular freshwater fish remain generally disregarded. These species, which may not flaunt the fabulousness their marine partners, assume imperative parts in keeping up with biological system wellbeing and working. From supplement cycling to controlling bug populaces, these fish add to the multifaceted snare of life in freshwater environments.

   1.2. The Compromised Variety

   Imperiled less popular freshwater fish address a microcosm of the more extensive biodiversity emergency confronting freshwater environments. The Worldwide Association for Preservation of Nature (IUCN) Red Rundown sorts numerous less popular species as imperiled or fundamentally jeopardized. The deficiency of these fish lessens the variety of freshwater life as well as disturbs the natural equilibrium, with potential far reaching influences all through the whole biological system.

2. **Dangers to Imperiled Less popular Freshwater Fish**
   2.1. Territory Annihilation and Adjustment
   One of the essential dangers to jeopardized less popular freshwater fish is living space obliteration and modification. Human exercises like dam development, urbanization, and agrarian extension frequently bring about the debasement and fracture of freshwater territories. These modifications upset regular stream streams, ruin movement examples, and breaking point reasonable rearing and taking care of justification for these species.

   2.2. Contamination: A Deadly Blend
   Contamination, originating from rural overflow, modern releases, and untreated sewage, represents a grave danger to the prosperity of freshwater fish. Raised degrees of supplements, synthetics, and contaminations debase water quality, affecting fish wellbeing, regenerative achievement, and in general endurance. The outcomes of contamination reach out past individual species to influence whole environments.

   2.3. Overfishing and Unreasonable Collecting
   Overfishing and unreasonable collecting rehearses compound the difficulties looked by imperiled less popular freshwater fish. These species are frequently focused on for the aquarium exchange, conventional medication, or as a food source. Unregulated fishing, combined with damaging stuff and catch of adolescents, prompts populace declines and, now and again, drives species to the edge of eradication.

   2.4. Intrusive Species: Quiet Trespassers

The presentation of intrusive species represents a huge danger to local freshwater fish. Obtrusive contenders and hunters can outcompete or go after imperiled species, prompting decreases in local populaces. Also, obtrusive species might present sicknesses that local fish need insusceptibility to, further compounding the dangers looked by jeopardized species.

2.5. Environmental Change: A Developing Danger

The effects of environmental change, including increasing temperatures, modified precipitation examples, and outrageous climate occasions, represent a developing hazard to freshwater fish. These progressions can upset the environmental equilibrium of amphibian biological systems, influencing the accessibility of food, reproducing conditions, and movement designs. Environmental change intensifies existing dangers and adds an extra layer of intricacy to the protection challenge.

3. **Notable Jeopardized Less popular Freshwater Fish Species**

   3.1. The Fiends Opening Pupfish (Cyprinodon diabolis)

   The Demons Opening Pupfish, endemic to a solitary area in Nevada's Villains Opening, remains as one of the most uncommon fish species on the planet. With a populace of less than 100 people, this small fish faces the inevitable danger of eradication. Natural surroundings annihilation, water extraction, and changes in water quality have driven the Villains Opening Pupfish to the edge, featuring the weakness of species limited to disengaged living spaces.

   3.2. The Humpback Chub (Gila cypha)

   Endemic to the Colorado Waterway bowl, the Humpback Chub is a remarkable and old fish species confronting significant dangers. Dam development, adjusted waterway streams, and rivalry with non-local species have added to the decay of this once-plentiful fish. Preservation endeavors, including territory reclamation and the evacuation of non-local hunters, are critical for forestalling the Humpback Chub's annihilation.

3.3. The Mekong Goliath Catfish (Pangasianodon gigas)

One of the biggest freshwater fish on the planet, the Mekong Goliath Catfish, is local to the Mekong Waterway in Southeast Asia. Overfishing, territory misfortune, and dam development along the Mekong Waterway present serious dangers to this notorious species. Preservation drives, remembering the foundation of safeguarded regions and guidelines for fishing rehearses, are basic for guaranteeing the endurance of the Mekong Monster Catfish.

3.4. The Vaquita (Phocoena sinus)

Albeit not a fish, the Vaquita, a little porpoise endemic to the Inlet of California, is significant of the difficulties looked by sea-going species. The Vaquita's populace has dove because of bycatch in unlawful gillnets used to get one more jeopardized animal categories, the totoaba fish. Pressing protection measures, including the implementation of fishing guidelines and the advancement of elective stuff, are fundamental to forestall the Vaquita's annihilation.

4. Preservation Procedures for Imperiled Less popular Freshwater Fish

4.1. Living space Insurance and Reclamation

The foundation of preservation endeavors for imperiled less popular freshwater fish lies in environment security and rebuilding. Laying out safeguarded regions, riparian cushion zones, and reestablishing debased living spaces add to the conservation of fundamental rearing and taking care of grounds.

Preservationists work to moderate the effects of dam development, carry out manageable land-use rehearses, and guarantee the free progression of waterways to help fish movement.

4.2. Feasible Fisheries The executives

Carrying out reasonable fisheries the executives rehearses is basic to address overfishing and unreasonable gathering. This includes setting get limits, directing stuff types, and authorizing occasional terminations to safeguard basic bringing forth regions. Local area based fisheries the executives, where nearby networks effectively partake in direction, cultivates a feeling of obligation and guarantees the drawn out manageability of fish populaces.

4.3. Obtrusive Species Control

Endeavors to control and oversee obtrusive species are imperative for safeguarding local freshwater fish. Destruction programs, natural surroundings rebuilding, and the improvement of early location frameworks add to limiting the effect of obtrusive contenders and hunters. Forestalling the presentation of non-local species through stricter guidelines likewise assumes an essential part in protection.

4.4. Environment Strong Protection Techniques

Adjusting protection systems to the difficulties presented by environmental change is fundamental. This includes distinguishing environment versatile living spaces, executing reclamation extends that record for evolving conditions, and creating systems to moderate the effects of outrageous climate occasions. Cooperative examination endeavors add to a superior comprehension of the particular weaknesses of jeopardized species to environmental change.

4.5. Public Mindfulness and Schooling

Raising public mindfulness about the significance of jeopardized less popular freshwater fish is a vital part of effective preservation. Instructive projects, outreach drives, and associations with neighborhood networks add to building support for preservation endeavors. Drawing in general society in resident science projects cultivates a feeling of association with these jeopardized species and energizes aggregate activity.

5. The Job of Regulation and Worldwide Coordinated effort

5.1. Reinforcing Lawful Insurances

Strong lawful systems are fundamental for the security of imperiled freshwater fish. Fortifying and implementing regulation that precludes territory obliteration, directs fishing practices, and addresses contamination are basic moves toward guaranteeing the endurance of these species.

Legitimate securities ought to stretch out to the environments these fish depend on, making a thorough way to deal with preservation.

5.2. Global Cooperation for Transboundary Species

Numerous freshwater fish species range different nations, requiring worldwide cooperation for successful preservation. Arrangements and settlements that work with collaboration among countries are essential for tending to transboundary preservation challenges. Shared liability and composed endeavors add to the protection of transitory courses, favorable places, and environments fundamental for the endurance of these species.

6. Protection Difficulties and the Way Forward

6.1. Restricted Assets and Subsidizing

Protection endeavors for imperiled less popular freshwater fish frequently face difficulties related with restricted assets and subsidizing. Contending needs and the eclipsing of freshwater environments add to an absence of venture. Activating monetary help, earning public and political consideration, and laying out inventive financing systems are fundamental stages to beat these difficulties.

6.2. Quickly Changing Scenes

The fast speed of improvement and land-use change represents a huge test to preservation endeavors. Staying up with these progressions and adjusting procedures to address arising dangers require readiness and proactive preparation. Incorporating preservation contemplations into land-use arranging and advancement choices is critical for guaranteeing the drawn out diligence of freshwater fish populaces.

6.3. Adjusting Protection and Human Requirements

Accomplishing a harmony between the protection of imperiled less popular freshwater fish and addressing the requirements of human populaces is a perplexing undertaking. Maintainable improvement that coordinates protection objectives, gives elective jobs to networks reliant upon fishing, and integrates the worth of freshwater environments into dynamic cycles is fundamental.

6.2 Success Stories in Conservation

Preservation endeavors, energized by committed people, associations, and networks, have yielded astounding examples of overcoming adversity in the mission to safeguard jeopardized species and save delicate environments. While various difficulties persevere, these examples of overcoming adversity give encouraging signs, exhibiting the positive effect that purposeful preservation activities can accomplish.

In this investigation, we dive into a few motivating examples of overcoming adversity that feature the strength of species on the edge and the groundbreaking force of preservation drives.

1. **The Bald Eagle (Haliaeetus leucocephalus): An Image of Versatility**

   Once wavering near the very edge of eradication, the Bald Eagle's story remains as a demonstration of the versatility of nature and the viability of protection endeavors. Boundless utilization of the pesticide DDT during the twentieth century prompted diminishing eggshells and regenerative disappointment in Bald Eagles, pushing them unsafely near annihilation. The restricting of DDT during the 1970s and thorough preservation measures, including natural surroundings security, hostage reproducing, and renewed introduction programs, prepared for a surprising recuperation.

   Today, the Bald Eagle populace in the US has taken off from a simple 417 reproducing matches in the mid 1960s to north of 9,700 rearing sets by 2006. Delisting the Bald Eagle from the Imperiled Species Act in 2007 denoted a memorable second, representing the fruitful recuperation of a public symbol. This example of overcoming adversity highlights the significance of designated preservation mediations, legitimate securities, and public mindfulness in resuscitating an animal types near the precarious edge of termination.

2. **The Bedouin Oryx (Oryx leucoryx): From Eradication to Renewed introduction**

   The Bedouin Oryx, a notorious image of the Middle Eastern Promontory, confronted termination in the wild during the last 50% of the twentieth 100 years due to overhunting and living space debasement. By the mid 1970s, the species was pronounced wiped out in nature. Nonetheless, purposeful endeavors drove by the Phoenix Zoo, the Fauna Protection Society, and the public authority of Oman started hostage rearing projects to save the Middle Eastern Oryx from blankness.

   Effective hostage rearing endeavors brought about a reasonable populace of Middle Eastern Oryx, and renewed introduction programs were sent off. The primary delivery happened in Oman in 1982, denoting a notable second as whenever a creature terminated in the wild first was once again introduced effectively. Ensuing renewed introductions happened in different nations across the Middle Eastern Promontory. Accordingly, the Middle Eastern Oryx, once pronounced terminated, presently meanders aimlessly in its local territories, exhibiting the potential for protection to switch the direst of conditions.

3. **The California Condor (Gymnogyps californianus): A Glorious Rebound**

   The California Condor, North America's biggest land bird, confronted approaching elimination in the late twentieth 100 years.

   Lead harming from ingesting spent lead ammo, natural surroundings annihilation, and microtrash ingestion compromised the couple of residual people. In 1987, confronting a populace of just 27 condors, protectionists went with a strong choice to catch all excess wild condors for a hostage rearing project.

   The escalated rearing endeavors that followed, combined with a lead ammo boycott in California's condor range, added to a sluggish yet consistent recuperation. Renewed introduction programs started during the 1990s, delivering hostage reproduced condors into nature. Starting around 2022, the California Condor populace has developed to north of 500 people, with over half taking off uninhibitedly in nature. This example of overcoming adversity highlights the complex dance of hostage rearing, environment the executives, and regulative activity in saving an animal categories from the verge of termination.

4. **The Iberian Lynx (Lynx pardinus): A Protection Win in Europe**

   The Iberian Lynx, the world's most jeopardized feline species, confronted a risky decay because of territory misfortune, prey shortage, and a decrease in bunny populaces, its essential food source. By the mid 2000s, the Iberian Lynx populace dwindled to less than 100 people, acquiring it the situation with the world's generally jeopardized cat.

   Protection endeavors initiated by the Spanish and Portuguese state run administrations, alongside NGOs, for example, the World Untamed life Asset (WWF), zeroed in on natural surroundings reclamation, hostage reproducing, and the renewed introduction of the lynx's essential prey, the European bunny. The Lynx Ex-Situ Preservation Program, including the reproducing of lynx in imprisonment, assumed a vital part in getting the species' future.

   Starting around 2022, the Iberian Lynx populace has bounced back to north of 1,100 people, stamping one of the best carnivore protection stories. The coordinated endeavors to address environment debasement, support prey populaces, and once again introduce hostage reproduced lynx into their normal living spaces feature the potential for switching the destiny of even the most fundamentally imperiled species.

5. **The Kakapo (Strigops habroptilus): A Parrot's Versatility**

   The Kakapo, a nighttime parrot local to New Zealand, confronted

| 123 |

a steep downfall with the presentation of intrusive species like rodents, stoats, and felines. By the 1990s, just 50 Kakapo people remained, making it perhaps of the most extraordinary bird on earth. In a final desperate attempt to save the species, all leftover Kakapo were moved to hunter free islands.

Escalated protection measures, including hunter control, living space rebuilding, and the execution of a strengthening taking care of program, added to the Kakapo's sluggish yet consistent recuperation. By 2019, the Kakapo populace had expanded to around 200 people.

While challenges continue, the Kakapo's versatility notwithstanding close annihilation highlights the significance of versatile preservation procedures customized to the extraordinary requirements of every species.

6. **The Dim Wolf (Canis lupus): A Preservation Achievement in Yellowstone**

The renewed introduction of the Dark Wolf to Yellowstone Public Park in the US in 1995 stands as an essential crossroads in preservation history. Many years of hunter control had extirpated the Dim Wolf from Yellowstone, prompting environmental irregular characteristics and a flowing impact on different species. Perceiving the significance of the wolf in keeping up with environment wellbeing, a renewed introduction program was started.

24 wolves were once again introduced to Yellowstone, prompting a groundbreaking biological shift known as trophic outpouring. The presence of wolves impacted the way of behaving of elk, which, thus, impacted plant populaces and the environment of different species. The recovery of willow and aspen trees, beforehand overgrazed by elk, affected larks, beavers, and other untamed life. This example of overcoming adversity represents the unpredictable associations inside biological systems and the job of dominant hunters in forming biodiversity.

7. **The Vaquita (Phocoena sinus): Pressing Preservation on the Edge**

While numerous protection examples of overcoming adversity move trust, a few animal types stay on the cliff of termination, requiring critical and supported endeavors. The Vaquita, a little porpoise endemic to the Inlet of California, is basically imperiled with a couple of people remaining. The essential danger to the Vaquita is unintentional snare in unlawful gillnets used to get one more imperiled animal categories, the totoaba fish.

Traditionalists, legislatures, and nearby networks are working enthusiastically to address this emergency. Drives incorporate the implementation of fishing guidelines, the improvement of elective fishing stuff, and worldwide coordinated effort to battle the unlawful exchange totoaba swim bladders. The Vaquita's story fills in as a distinct sign of the direness and intricacy of protection endeavors expected to save species on the verge.

8. **Illustrations Learned and Future Yearnings**

These examples of overcoming adversity highlight a few basic illustrations in preservation. Right off the bat, versatile administration and an eagerness to pursue strong choices, like hostage rearing and renewed introduction, are fundamental devices in the protection tool stash. Also, the interconnectedness of biological systems features the significance of tending to underlying drivers and grasping the more extensive natural setting.

Thirdly, the job of lawful securities, local area commitment, and worldwide joint effort couldn't possibly be more significant in that frame of mind for effective protection results.

Planning ahead, preservation endeavors should keep on developing because of arising difficulties, for example, environmental change, living space debasement, and the unlawful natural life exchange. Creative advancements, resident science drives, and interdisciplinary joint effort offer promising roads for propelling preservation objectives. At last, the examples of overcoming adversity featured here act as encouraging signs, rousing an aggregate obligation to saving biodiversity, safeguarding imperiled species, and cultivating an agreeable concurrence among humankind and the regular world.

6.3 How Individuals Can Contribute to Conservation

Preservation is an aggregate liability that rises above borders, including states, associations, and networks. Nonetheless, the force of individual commitments ought to be acknowledged with a sober mind. Each individual has the ability to put forth a significant effect on protection attempts. In this investigation, we dive into different ways people can add to preservation, encouraging a feeling of stewardship for the planet's biodiversity.

1. Develop Ecological Mindfulness: The Groundwork of Preservation

Ecological mindfulness shapes the bedrock of individual commitments to preservation. Grasping the interconnectedness of biological systems, the significance of biodiversity, and the dangers confronting the regular world enables people to go with informed decisions. This mindfulness can be developed through schooling, commitment with ecological issues, and remaining informed about current preservation challenges.

2. Maintainable Way of life Decisions: Lessening Environmental Impressions

Embracing a practical way of life is quite possibly of the most effective way people can add to protection. This includes settling on decisions that limit natural effect, for example, decreasing energy and water utilization, embracing eco-accommodating items, and rehearsing dependable waste administration. Basic activities like utilizing reusable packs, lessening single-use plastics, and picking energy-effective machines all in all add to a more practical future.

3. Supporting Protection Associations: An Aggregate Exertion

Supporting protection associations is an immediate way for people to add to bigger scope endeavors. Gifts to legitimate associations can subsidize basic examination, living space rebuilding ventures, and local area based protection drives. By lining up with associations that share their qualities, people become basic accomplices in the worldwide preservation development.

4. Taking part in Resident Science: Bridling Aggregate Information

Resident science drives influence the aggregate force of people to accumulate information and add to logical examination. Stages like eBird, iNaturalist, and Zooniverse permit individuals to record perceptions of untamed life, contributing significant data to scientists. Participating in resident science advances logical comprehension as well as cultivates a feeling of association with the normal world.

5. Instructing and Pushing: Enhancing Protection Messages

Schooling and promotion are strong devices for people to intensify preservation messages. Sharing information about ecological issues, the significance of biodiversity, and noteworthy stages for preservation makes an expanding influence. People can take part in conversations inside their networks, schools, and groups of friends, igniting discussions that lead to expanded mindfulness and aggregate activity.

6. Dependable Diversion: Appreciating Nature Without Hurting It

Taking part in mindful entertainment guarantees that people can appreciate nature without hurting. This incorporates following Leave No Follow standards, regarding natural life territories, and sticking to moral untamed life watching rehearses. Mindful entertainment cultivates an agreeable connection among people and the normal world, limiting pessimistic effects on biological systems.

7. Advancing Reasonable The travel industry: Supporting Protection through Investigation

Picking supportable the travel industry choices adjusts travel to protection objectives. This includes choosing eco-accommodating facilities, supporting neighborhood protection drives, and selecting visit administrators focused on moral and manageable practices. Manageable the travel industry limits the ecological effect of movement as well as adds to the conservation of regular and social legacy.

8. Cultivating for Untamed life: Making Territory Asylums

Cultivating for untamed life changes individual spaces into safe houses for biodiversity. Establishing local species, giving water sources, and making cover spaces add to nearby biological systems. People can likewise take part in local area cultivating projects, making interconnected green spaces that help different plant and creature species.

9. Picking Economical Items: Force of Customer Decisions

Settling on manageable buyer decisions conveys strong messages to ventures. Choosing items that are morally obtained, harmless to the ecosystem, and have insignificant natural effect urges organizations to embrace economical practices.

By supporting organizations with solid ecological responsibilities, people add to a market shift toward more mindful creation.

10. Diminishing Meat Utilization: An Eating regimen that welcomes environments

Lessening meat utilization is a dietary decision that can decidedly influence the climate. The animals business is a critical supporter of deforestation, territory misfortune, and ozone depleting substance emanations. Embracing plant-based or flexitarian slims down mitigates these effects and advances more reasonable food frameworks.

11. Chipping in for Protection: Active Association

Chipping in for preservation projects furnishes people with active contribution in safeguarding normal living spaces. Whether taking part in tree-establishing drives, natural life observing projects, or ocean side cleanups, chipping in encourages an immediate association with preservation endeavors and fabricates a feeling of obligation for the climate.

12. Becoming Educated Shoppers: Requesting Responsibility

Being educated shoppers includes exploring the natural acts of organizations and considering them responsible. People can pick items from organizations focused on manageability and utilize their buying ability to help organizations that focus on preservation and moral practices.

13. Supporting for Strategy Change: Impacting Foundational Activity

Pushing for strategy change is a significant road for people to impact foundational activity. Drawing in with neighborhood and public policymakers, supporting harmless to the ecosystem approaches, and taking part in promotion crusades add to molding administrative systems that focus on preservation.

14. Taking part in Rebuilding Undertakings: Recuperating the Land

Taking part in territory reclamation projects permits people to add to the recuperating of corrupted environments straightforwardly. Whether establishing trees, reestablishing wetlands, or tidying up dirtied regions, reclamation endeavors emphatically affect the versatility of normal living spaces.

15. Cultivating a Protection Outlook: Supporting Future Stewards

Cultivating a preservation mentality in more youthful ages guarantees the congruity of endeavors to safeguard the climate. Guardians, teachers, and local area pioneers assume an imperative part in imparting upsides of ecological obligation, interest in nature, and a feeling of stewardship in kids and youthful grown-ups.

Chapter 7

Citizen Science and Research Opportunities

In the many-sided snare of logical investigation, a progressive organization has arisen — the coordinated effort between proficient specialists and energetic residents, a peculiarity known as resident science. This collusion rises above customary limits, engaging people to add to logical undertakings and cultivating a more profound association among science and society effectively. This complete investigation digs into the unique domain of resident science, disentangling its beginnings, framing its assorted applications, and enlightening the bunch potential open doors it presents for the two scientists and the drew in broad daylight.

2. The Development of Resident Science

2.1. Beginnings and Verifiable Setting

The foundations of resident science follow back hundreds of years, with beginner naturalists and lovers adding to the comprehension of the normal world. Trailblazers like Charles Darwin depended on the perceptions of resident researchers to shape historic hypotheses. Over the long run, mechanical headways, especially in correspondence and information assortment, play enhanced the part of residents in logical revelation.

2.2. Mechanical Impetuses

The coming of computerized innovations has been a distinct advantage, pushing resident science into another period. Online stages, portable applications, and interconnected data sets work with consistent joint effort and information sharing. These mechanical apparatuses make investment more open as well as improve the quality and amount of information gathered.

2.3. Democratization of Information

Resident science exemplifies the democratization of information, separating the conventional ordered progressions in logical examination. It enables people from different foundations to add to projects spreading over a wide exhibit of disciplines, from cosmology and biology to hereditary qualities and then some. This democratization encourages inclusivity, guaranteeing that logical request mirrors the wealth of human encounters and viewpoints.

3. The Variety of Resident Science Activities

3.1. Stargazing and Astronomy

Resident researchers play played essential parts in cosmic disclosures. Projects like Zooniverse's System Zoo influence the aggregate force of workers to order universes, adding to how we might interpret the immense universe. Beginners have likewise made huge commitments to distinguishing transient heavenly occasions, for example, supernovae and comets.

3.2. Nature and Biodiversity Checking

In the domain of nature, resident science projects center around checking biodiversity and following the wellbeing of biological systems. Drives like eBird and iNaturalist draw in birdwatchers and nature lovers in reporting bird sightings and plant and creature perceptions. These commitments help scientists in concentrating on species disseminations, movement designs, and the effects of environmental change on biodiversity.

3.3. Natural Protection and Contamination Observing

Resident researchers effectively take part in ecological protection by checking contamination levels and adding to territory reclamation. Projects like the Incomparable Lakes Ocean side Wellbeing Checking System include volunteers in evaluating water quality, assisting with distinguishing possible dangers to sea-going environments.

3.4. Wellbeing and Medication

In the field of wellbeing and medication, resident researchers add to explore on illnesses and general wellbeing. Stages like Foldit draw in gamers in tackling complex protein-collapsing issues, possibly supporting the improvement of new medications. Furthermore, people can partake in projects zeroed in on following sickness episodes or contemplating the microbiome.

3.5. Verifiable and Social Exploration

Resident science stretches out its compass to authentic and social examination. Drives like Translate Bentham call upon volunteers to decipher and digitize authentic compositions, adding to the conservation of social legacy. This crossing point of resident science with history and culture features its adaptability in different spaces.

4. The Course of Resident Science

4.1. Project Plan and Inception

The inception of a resident science project starts with cautious undertaking plan. Analysts frame the objectives, strategies, and expected results, guaranteeing that the venture lines up with both logical targets and the abilities of resident members. Clear correspondence and openness are foremost at this stage.

4.2. Enlistment and Preparing

Enlistment of resident researchers includes contacting networks through different channels, including on the web stages, public venues, and instructive foundations. Instructional meetings are led to acquaint members with project goals, information assortment techniques, and a particular conventions. This stage stresses the significance of normalized strategies to keep up with information quality.

4.3. Information Assortment and Accommodation

The core of resident science lies in information assortment. Members, outfitted with rules and apparatuses, contribute perceptions, estimations, or characterizations. Computerized stages smooth out information accommodation, guaranteeing an incorporated store that works with investigation. Continuous information section upgrades the promptness and significance of the undertaking.

4.4. Quality Affirmation and Approval

Keeping up with information precision is basic in resident science. Quality affirmation conventions, including information approval processes, are laid out to confirm the dependability of resident contributed data. Analysts frequently execute governing rules to guarantee that the information lines up with logical guidelines.

4.5. Information Examination and Translation

When the information is gathered, the insightful stage starts. Specialists utilize factual strategies, AI calculations, or other applicable apparatuses to dissect the information. The coordinated effort between proficient researchers and resident donors frequently prompts a multi-layered understanding of results, improving the exploration with different points of view.

4.6. Correspondence of Results

An essential part of resident science is the straightforward and corresponding correspondence of results. Analysts share discoveries with members, recognizing their commitments. This correspondence encourages a feeling of achievement among resident researchers, building up their job as dynamic accomplices in the logical cycle.

5. Advantages and Open doors for Analysts

5.1. Information Adaptability and Geographic Inclusion

One of the essential benefits of resident science for scientists is the capacity to increase information assortment. The sheer number of members takes into account broad inclusion, empowering undertakings to accumulate information over huge geographic regions and expanded time spans. This adaptability is especially worthwhile in fields like environment, where thorough informational indexes are significant for figuring out biological systems.

5.2. Cost-Adequacy

Resident science projects frequently end up being practical contrasted with conventional examination techniques. The dispersed idea of information assortment decreases the requirement for broad hands on work by proficient researchers. Furthermore, the cooperative model limits the costs related with employing enormous examination groups.

5.3. Local area Commitment and Public Effort

Drawing in with resident researchers works with direct local area association in research drives. This commitment fabricates an extension among specialists and people in general, cultivating a feeling of shared liability regarding logical investigation. Through cooperation in projects, people foster a more profound comprehension of logical cycles and add to the more extensive dispersal of logical information.

5.4. Admittance to Different Ranges of abilities

The contribution of resident researchers brings a variety of assorted ranges of abilities to investigate projects. Members might have skill in fields like innovation, training, or local area arranging. This variety enhances the examination cycle, giving reciprocal points of view and abilities that may not be available in a conventional exploration group.

5.5. Long haul Observing and Information Coherence

Resident science projects frequently benefit from supported commitment, taking into consideration long haul observing of biological or ecological changes. This drawn out interest adds to information progression, giving important bits of knowledge into patterns and examples over the long run. Scientists can use this worldly aspect for additional vigorous investigations and a more profound comprehension of dynamic environments.

6. Advantages and Potential open doors for Resident Researchers

6.1. Mastering and Ability Advancement

Taking part in resident science offers people the chance to extend their insight and foster new abilities. Members gain active involvement with logical approaches, information assortment, and examination. This experiential learning adds to logical education and encourages a feeling of interest and investigation.

6.2. Association with Nature and Local area

Taking part in resident science projects associates people to the regular world and their neighborhood networks. Whether through birdwatching, environmental studies, or different exercises, members foster a feeling of spot and a comprehension of the biological systems in which they live. This association cultivates a more profound appreciation for the climate and a feeling of local area among members.

6.3. Commitment to Logical Disclosure

One of the most compensating perspectives for resident researchers is the amazing chance to add to logical revelation effectively. Whether it's distinguishing another species, reporting an uncommon way of behaving, or adding to a leap forward in understanding, members become fundamental supporters of the progression of information.

6.4. Individual Strengthening and Support

Commitment to resident science engages people by showing the way that they can assume a significant part in tending to logical difficulties. This strengthening frequently stretches out past the domain of science, encouraging a feeling of organization and support for natural and cultural issues. Resident researchers become diplomats for the causes they support.

6.5. Local area Building and Social Communication

Taking part in resident science sets out open doors for local area building and social cooperation. Whether on the web or face to face, the common quest for logical objectives unites individuals, encouraging a feeling of kinship. This social angle adds to the maintainability and outcome of resident science drives.

7. Difficulties and Contemplations

7.1. Information Quality and Normalization

Keeping up with information quality in resident science projects is a relentless test. Changes in member aptitude, hardware, and adherence to conventions can present irregularities. Laying out strong quality affirmation systems and clear information guidelines is essential to address these difficulties.

7.2. Member Inspiration and Maintenance

Supporting member inspiration over the drawn out presents a test. Factors, for example, project plan, correspondence systems, and acknowledgment of commitments impact member commitment. Methodologies to improve inspiration and maintenance might incorporate giving clear objectives, offering criticism, and recognizing the effect of individual commitments.

7.3. Moral Contemplations and Informed Assent

Moral contemplations in resident science include issues of security, assent, and information proprietorship. Clear rules for informed assent, particularly in projects including touchy information, are fundamental. Laying out straightforward correspondence channels and regarding the freedoms of members are basic moral standards.

7.4. Openness and Inclusivity

Guaranteeing the openness and inclusivity of resident science projects is basic. Hindrances connected with innovation, language, geology, and financial elements can restrict cooperation. Endeavors to address these boundaries might incorporate giving multilingual assets, offering assorted cooperation choices, and taking into account the requirements of different networks.

7.5. Mix with Customary Exploration

Powerful incorporation of resident science with conventional exploration rehearses is a continuous test. Overcoming any barrier between proficient specialists and resident researchers requires open correspondence, shared regard, and an acknowledgment of the one of a kind qualities each brings to the coordinated effort. Laying out clear jobs and assumptions adds to an agreeable organization.

8. Future Bearings and Arising Patterns
8.1. Propels in Innovation

The proceeded with headway of innovation will shape the eventual fate of resident science. Developments in sensors, information examination, and man-made brainpower will improve the productivity and exactness of information assortment and investigation. Wearable gadgets, portable applications, and brilliant sensors will additionally democratize cooperation in logical exploration.

8.2. Worldwide Coordinated effort and Systems administration

The potential for worldwide coordinated effort in resident science is immense. Organizing stages that interface members, scientists, and associations worldwide will work with information trade and cooperative activities. This interconnected methodology will add to a more complete comprehension of worldwide logical difficulties.

8.3. Instruction and Educational plan Coordination

The combination of resident science into training educational plans will assume a urgent part in supporting another age of logically proficient people. Resident science projects intended for schools and instructive establishments give involved opportunities for growth, encouraging a feeling of interest and request.

8.4. Strategy and Institutional Help

Strong arrangement systems and institutional help are fundamental for additional standard resident science. Approaches that perceive and boost the commitments of resident researchers, safeguard their privileges, and guarantee information security will support the development of resident science drives. Institutional help can appear through subsidizing, framework, and acknowledgment.

8.5. Public Mindfulness and Commitment

Lifting public mindfulness and commitment to resident science is significant for its proceeded with progress. Outreach crusades, local area occasions, and media drives can feature the effect of resident science on logical headways and stress the openness of interest. Building a culture of resident commitment to logical undertakings will be vital.

9. Contextual investigations: Representing the Effect of Resident Science

9.1. The Incomparable Patio Bird Count

The Incomparable Patio Bird Count is a perfect representation of a resident science drive with worldwide effect. Sent off in 1998, this yearly occasion empowers birdwatchers, everything being equal, to include and report bird sightings in their neighborhoods. The aggregate information adds to how we might interpret bird movement designs, populace elements, and the effect of environmental change on avian species.

9.2. Project Squirrel

Project Squirrel represents how resident science can add to natural exploration. Begun in the Chicago region, this undertaking welcomes members to notice and archive squirrel conduct. The information gathered has given experiences into the flexibility of squirrel populaces in metropolitan conditions, adding to how we might interpret metropolitan biology.

9.3. Foldit: Gamers Unwinding Protein Designs

Foldit bridles the force of gaming to take care of mind boggling logical issues. In this resident science project, gamers contend to foresee protein structures, adding to explore on illnesses and medication improvement. The game's prosperity features the creative manners by which resident science can use assorted abilities and interests.

9.4. The Lost Ladybug Undertaking

The Lost Ladybug Undertaking connects with resident researchers, especially youngsters, in the documentation of ladybug species. Members submit photos of ladybugs they experience, adding to investigate on the dissemination and overflow of these bugs. This task features how resident science can be intended to include different age gatherings and cultivate an association with nature since early on.

7.1 Involving the Public in Studying Lesser-Known Species

The investigation of less popular species, frequently eclipsed by additional magnetic partners, presents an extraordinary arrangement of difficulties and potential open doors. While these species assume critical parts in environments, their unnoticeable nature and restricted perceivability can block conventional exploration endeavors. Lately, there has been a change in perspective in logical request, with the mix of resident science ways to deal with include general society in concentrating on less popular species. This cooperative model tends to the holes in information assortment as well as cultivates a feeling of local area commitment, logical education, and natural stewardship. In this investigation, we dive into the meaning of including people in general in the investigation of less popular species, the development of resident science in this specific circumstance, and the bunch ways people add to logical comprehension.

2. The Meaning of Less popular Species in Biological systems
2.1. Natural Jobs

Less popular species, however frequently ignored, assume vital parts in biological systems. From supplement cycling to keeping up with natural equilibrium, these species add to the complex trap of life. Nonetheless, because of their careful propensities, restricted geological appropriation, or little populace sizes, they much of the time escape the spotlight in logical exploration.

2.2. Biodiversity Preservation

Understanding and preserving less popular species is indispensable to biodiversity protection. The deficiency of any species, no matter what its perceivability, can upset the fragile equilibrium of biological systems. Less popular species might have extraordinary variations, hereditary variety, or cooperative connections that add to the general flexibility and strength of biological systems.

3. The Development of Resident Science
3.1. From Beginners to Teammates

By and large, beginners and naturalists have made critical commitments to the investigation of nature. The coming of formalized resident science addresses an organized and cooperative way to deal with including people in general in logical exploration. The ascent of computerized innovation and online stages has democratized the logical cycle, empowering people to take part in information assortment, examination, and, surprisingly, the plan of exploration questions.

3.2. Growing Exploration Limits

Resident science grows the limits of logical exploration by utilizing the aggregate force of a different and geologically boundless local area. This approach takes into consideration the assortment of immense datasets that would be strategically difficult or monetarily impossible for conventional exploration groups to assemble alone. With regards to concentrating on less popular species, resident science turns into a competitive edge, upgrading the degree and profundity of examination.

4. Resident Science and Less popular Species: A Cooperative Relationship

4.1. Connecting with General society in Species Distinguishing proof

Less popular species frequently present difficulties in distinguishing proof, in any event, for prepared researchers. Resident science activities can connect with general society during the time spent species ID through easy to understand stages and versatile applications. These devices give an extension between logical skill and the energy of general society, empowering non-specialists to contribute important information on less popular species.

4.2. Local area Drove Protection Drives

Resident science goes past information assortment; it enables networks to play a functioning job in the protection of less popular species. Neighborhood people group, personally associated with their regular environmental factors, can contribute significant experiences, conventional information, and on-the-ground perceptions. This cooperative methodology encourages a feeling of pride and obligation regarding the preservation of less popular species.

4.3. Building Logical Proficiency

Support in resident science projects improves logical proficiency among the general population. By including people in the logical cycle, these tasks demystify research techniques, advance a more profound comprehension of biological ideas, and develop a feeling of natural stewardship.

Deductively educated networks are better prepared to see the value in the meaning of less popular species and supporter for their preservation.

4.4. Democratizing Preservation Endeavors

Resident science democratizes preservation endeavors, making it open to a more extensive segment. This inclusivity is especially essential for the investigation of less popular species, as it differentiates the pool of onlookers and information supporters. Individuals from different foundations, including those without formal logical preparation, can effectively take part in protection drives, encouraging a feeling of shared liability regarding biodiversity.

5. Examples of overcoming adversity in Resident Science and Less popular Species Exploration

5.1. The Incomparable Lawn Bird Count

The Incomparable Lawn Bird Count is an exemplary illustration of a resident science project that has contributed fundamentally to how we might interpret avian biodiversity. Members from around the world, going from prepared ornithologists to patio aficionados, meet up every year to count and report bird sightings. This task not just gathers important information on normal bird species yet in addition gives bits of knowledge into the appropriation and conduct of less popular avian species.

5.2. iNaturalist and Biodiversity Disclosure

iNaturalist, a famous resident science stage, permits clients to report and share perceptions of plants, creatures, and parasites. The stage utilizes picture acknowledgment innovation to aid species ID. This task has prompted the disclosure and documentation of various less popular species, including bugs, growths, and plants, improving comprehension we might interpret biodiversity.

5.3. The Lost Ladybug Venture

Zeroing in on a gathering of frequently neglected bugs, the Lost Ladybug Task urges members to report ladybug sightings. This task not just adds as far as anyone is concerned of ladybug variety yet in addition reveals insight into the appropriation and populaces of less popular ladybug species. Members, going from younger students to grown-ups, effectively participate in the revelation and preservation of these gainful bugs.

5.4. eBird and Avian Relocations

eBird, a resident science project committed to birding, has changed the manner in which we grasp avian movements. By amassing a large number of bird perceptions, eBird has worked with the following of transient examples, visit areas, and changes in circulation. This abundance of information has not just high level our insight into normal transitory species yet has additionally uncovered bits of knowledge into the developments of less popular and subtle birds.

6. Beating Difficulties in Resident Science and Less popular Species Exploration

6.1. Species Recognizable proof and Master Check

One of the essential difficulties in resident science including less popular species is the exactness of species recognizable proof. To address this, projects frequently consolidate master check processes. Innovation, like picture acknowledgment calculations and online discussions for cooperative distinguishing proof, can improve the precision of species ID by including both resident researchers and specialists.

6.2. Information Quality and Normalization

Guaranteeing the quality and normalization of information is urgent for its logical worth. Resident science projects utilize different techniques, for example, information approval conventions, normalized perception structures, and clear information accommodation rules, to keep up with information trustworthiness. Constant observing and input systems likewise add to working on the general nature of information gathered by members.

6.3. Inspiration and Supported Cooperation

Supporting inspiration and commitment among resident researchers over the long haul can challenge. Perceiving and compensating members, giving customary reports on project results, and encouraging a feeling of local area among patrons can add to supported interest and contribution. Projects that effectively include members in the logical cycle, like information examination and understanding, additionally improve inspiration.

6.4. Tending to Predisposition and Information Holes

Resident science undertakings might display predispositions with regards to geographic inclusion, species inclinations, or perception recurrence. To address these predispositions, drives frequently consolidate designated outreach procedures to draw in different networks. Projects that unequivocally center around less popular species can assist with filling information holes and give a more far reaching comprehension of biodiversity.

7. Future Bearings and Advancements

7.1. Joining of Innovation

The joining of innovation, including man-made consciousness, AI, and portable applications, keeps on upgrading the adequacy of resident science.

Robotized species ID apparatuses, continuous information assortment, and intelligent versatile stages are propelling the field, making it more available and proficient for members.

7.2. Worldwide Coordinated efforts and Organizations

The eventual fate of resident science lies in worldwide joint efforts and organizations. Interfacing members and tasks across borders encourages an aggregate way to deal with concentrating on less popular species. Worldwide joint efforts empower the pooling of different information, assets, and mastery, adding to a more comprehensive comprehension of worldwide biodiversity.

7.3. Instructive Reconciliation

Coordinating resident science into formal and casual school systems addresses a strong road for sustaining the up and coming age of researchers and ecological stewards. Instructive foundations can use resident science tasks to improve experiential learning, advance logical request, and impart a feeling of obligation for the regular world.

7.4. Strategy and Protection Effect

As resident science keeps on producing powerful datasets, its likely effect on arrangement and protection choices turns out to be progressively critical. Drawing in policymakers and preservation specialists with resident science results can impact the improvement of preservation procedures, safeguarded region the executives, and the prioritization of less popular species in protection drives.

7.2 Collaborative Efforts with Scientists and Researchers

Cooperative endeavors between resident researchers and expert specialists address a dynamic and harmonious relationship that improves the profundity and extent of logical request. As resident science acquires noticeable quality in natural and biodiversity research, the coordinated effort with researchers brings an abundance of advantages.

Proficient analysts bring significant mastery, guaranteeing the logical meticulousness and exactness of information gathered through resident science drives. Their direction is instrumental in planning hearty exploration conventions, tending to strategic difficulties, and giving master confirmation to species recognizable proof. This cooperation guarantees that the information created by resident researchers satisfy logical guidelines, adding to tenable and dependable logical results.

Furthermore, researchers give a structure to deciphering and contextualizing the information inside the more extensive logical scene. Their capacity to blend data, recognize examples, and reach significant inferences adds profundity to the aggregate comprehension of less popular species and biological systems.

On the other hand, resident researchers bring energy, neighborhood information, and sheer numbers to the cooperative table. Their different foundations, going from novice naturalists to local area individuals personally associated with their nearby surroundings, offer an expansive range of perceptions. This inclusivity in information assortment helps fill geological holes and gives bits of knowledge into species conduct, conveyance, and biology that may be provoking for proficient specialists to exhaustively catch.

This cooperation cultivates a feeling of shared proprietorship and obligation regarding the normal world, enabling people to add to logical disclosure and preservation endeavors effectively. The aggregate effect of cooperative undertakings between resident researchers and scientists intensifies the ability to address squeezing environmental difficulties and adds to a more all encompassing comprehension of the mind boggling snare of life on The planet.

7.3 The Role of Technology in Discovering and Documenting Hidden Treasures

In the journey to find and record stowed away fortunes, innovation has arisen as a strong partner, changing the manner in which we investigate, notice, and grasp the normal world. From state of the art imaging advancements to modern information examination, the combination of innovation has opened new wildernesses in revealing the secrets of less popular species. This article investigates the multi-layered job of innovation in the revelation and documentation of stowed away fortunes, revealing insight into the groundbreaking effect of development on biodiversity research.

1. **High level Imaging Innovations**
   1.1. Camera Traps and Remote Detecting
   One of the momentous advancements in biodiversity research is the utilization of camera traps and remote detecting gadgets. Put decisively in the wild, camera traps catch slippery species in their regular environments, giving remarkable bits of knowledge into conduct, populace elements, and conveyance. Remote detecting advancements, for example, satellite symbolism and robots, offer an elevated perspective of scenes, supporting the ID of stowed away biological systems and species-rich regions that might be trying to get to.

1.2. DNA Barcoding and Metabarcoding

Progressions in atomic science have brought about DNA barcoding and metabarcoding procedures. These methodologies permit scientists to recognize species by examining their DNA, even from follow measures of natural material. DNA barcoding is especially valuable for affirming species characters, while metabarcoding empowers the concurrent recognizable proof of different species inside a given example. These advancements assume an essential part in finding mysterious species and grasping the perplexing connections inside biological systems.

2. Resident Science Stages and Portable Applications
2.1. iNaturalist and eBird

The ascent of resident science stages, like iNaturalist and eBird, has changed the scene of biodiversity information assortment. These versatile applications enable people to add to logical exploration by recording perceptions of widely varied vegetation. The easy to use interfaces, combined with picture acknowledgment calculations, empower general society to partake effectively in species ID and circulation planning. This cooperative methodology improves information assortment as well as democratizes the revelation of stowed away fortunes, as devotees overall become necessary supporters of logical undertakings.

2.2. Publicly supported Information and AI

Publicly supported information, produced by resident researchers, are progressively being tackled to prepare AI calculations. These calculations can then independently break down tremendous datasets, recognizing examples, species, and peculiarities. The marriage of resident science and AI speeds up the speed of revelation, permitting specialists to filter through broad information all the more proficiently and uncover stowed away fortunes that could have evaded conventional strategies.

3. Huge Information Examination and Computational Apparatuses

3.1. Information Incorporation and Investigation

The deluge of information from different sources requires progressed computational devices for incorporation and examination. Enormous information investigation empower analysts to combine data from assorted datasets, uncovering complex environmental connections and examples. By handling enormous volumes of information, researchers can distinguish stowed away fortunes, like interesting species or exceptional biological systems, and recognize the basic elements forming their reality.

3.2. Prescient Demonstrating and GIS

Geographic Data Frameworks (GIS) combined with prescient demonstrating instruments permit scientists to expect the presence of stowed away fortunes in view of natural factors. These instruments can anticipate reasonable natural surroundings, movement courses, and potential biodiversity areas of interest, directing scientists to explicit regions for designated investigation. Prescient demonstrating upgrades the productivity of field undertakings, improving the probability of finding less popular species.

4. Natural DNA (eDNA) Examining

Natural DNA (eDNA) testing has arisen as a harmless and exceptionally delicate procedure for recognizing stowed away species. This technique includes separating DNA sections shed by creatures into their current circumstance, like water or soil. By dissecting eDNA, analysts can recognize the presence of species without direct perception. This innovation is especially important for oceanic conditions, where tricky species might leave negligible follows yet at the same time contribute fundamentally to biological system elements.

5. Computer generated Reality (VR) and Increased Reality (AR)

5.1. Virtual Field Undertakings

Computer generated Reality (VR) and Increased Reality (AR) innovations are growing the limits of investigation by offering vivid encounters. Scientists and people in general can set out on virtual field endeavors, investigating distant living spaces and experiencing stowed away fortunes without truly being available. This works with logical effort and schooling as well as considers virtual revelation and documentation of species in their regular habitats.

6. **Challenges and Moral Contemplations**

While innovation has introduced another time of disclosure, it isn't without challenges and moral contemplations. The dependence on innovation ought to be offset with customary hands on work to guarantee the exactness and culmination of information. Also, issues connected with information protection, calculation predispositions, and the likely environmental effect of innovation should be painstakingly addressed to keep up with the respectability of biodiversity research.

Chapter 8

Uncovering the Stories

In the tremendous embroidery of human life, stories weave the strings of our common history, culture, and understanding. Uncovering these accounts is an excursion that rises above reality, digging into the rich embroidery of stories that characterize what our identity is. From the old legends to contemporary stories, the mission to uncover these accounts is an investigation that unfurls across different areas, including writing, history, paleontology, and the sky is the limit from there. This paper sets out on a far reaching investigation of the most common way of revealing stories, looking at the techniques, importance, and the groundbreaking force of narrating.

1. **The Antiquarianism of Stories**
  1. **Unearthing the Past**
  Prehistoric studies remains as a central strategy in revealing the tales of civilizations a distant memory. The careful removal of relics, translating antiquated scripts, and sorting out pieces of earthenware disclose the accounts of past social orders. Every

relic tells a quiet story, and the excavator turns into a narrator, reproducing the past through the remainders abandoned.

2. **Lost Urban areas and Failed to remember Civilizations**

Uncovering lost urban communities and failed to remember developments is a stunning part of archeological narrating. From the secretive Machu Picchu to the cryptic Mohenjo-daro, these old districts tell stories of cultural designs, mechanical progressions, and the recurring pattern of human life. The quiet stones and disintegrating walls become parts in the story of human development.

II. **Scholarly Investigation**

1. **Words as Windows**
   Writing fills in as a significant mode for revealing stories. Through the composed word, writers transport perusers into domains of creative mind, offering looks into assorted societies, verifiable periods, and the profundities of the human mind. Books, sonnets, and plays become entries through which perusers leave on excursions of disclosure, interfacing with characters and accounts that resound across time.
2. **Subtext and Imagery**

Revealing stories in writing frequently includes deciphering subtext and imagery. Scholars insert layers of significance underneath the surface, welcoming perusers to dive past the plot. The investigation of images, illustrations, and purposeful anecdotes is a course of uncovering stowed away stories inside the story, uncovering the nuanced viewpoints and more profound insights the creator looks to convey.

III. **Oral Customs and Legends**

1. **Passing Down Shrewdness**
   Oral customs and fables address a living vault of stories went down through ages. Inside these stories lie the aggregate insight,

convictions, and upsides of networks. The narrator turns into a caretaker of social legacy, and the demonstration of sharing stories orally guarantees the progression of customs, interfacing the present to the genealogical past.

2. **Social Variety**

The investigation of oral customs divulges the mind boggling variety of human societies. From the incredible adventures of the Nordic people groups to the mind boggling legends of Native people group, every oral practice adds an extraordinary part to the worldwide story. Revealing these accounts jelly social lavishness as well as cultivates diverse comprehension.

IV. Authentic Stories

1. **Archiving the Past**
   The discipline of history fills in as a formalized exertion in uncovering and recording stories from an earlier time. Through careful exploration, antiquarians piece together occasions, philosophies, and the cultural elements that have formed mankind's set of experiences. Essential sources, authentic reports, and onlooker accounts add to building stories that enlighten the intricacies of past times.
2. **Revisionist Chronicles**

Revealing stories in history is a continuous cycle set apart by the returning to and amendment of laid out accounts. The rise of revisionist accounts difficulties laid out standards, offering elective points of view and stories that were recently underestimated or overlooked. This powerful way to deal with verifiable narrating guarantees a more comprehensive and nuanced comprehension of the past.

V. Innovative Accounts

1. **Computerized Documents and Augmented Realities**
   The advanced age has introduced creative approaches to uncovering stories. Computerized chronicles safeguard verifiable reports, photos, and accounts, making them open to a worldwide crowd. Augmented reality advances empower clients to step into authentic settings, giving vivid encounters that rejuvenate stories in manners already unbelievable.
2. **The Effect of Virtual Entertainment**

Virtual entertainment stages have democratized narrating, permitting people to share individual stories, encounters, and points of view on a worldwide scale. From Twitter strings reporting regular day to day existence to Instagram stories catching critical minutes, the computerized scene has turned into an embroidery of interconnected stories, forming aggregate stories progressively.

VI. Individual Stories and Journals

1. **The Private Account**
   Revealing stories reaches out to the profoundly private domain of diaries and self-portrayals. People become the creators of their own accounts, sharing cozy subtleties of their lives, battles, and wins. These individual stories add to a more extensive comprehension of the human experience, cultivating sympathy and association among different crowds.
2. **Uncovering Stowed away Voices**

Diaries and individual stories likewise act as a stage for divulging stowed away voices and minimized viewpoints. Stories that were once consigned to the edges of standard talk view a space as heard, testing cultural standards and adding to a more comprehensive story scene.

8.1 Interviews with Biologists and Conservationists

The area of science and preservation is an embroidery of investigation, disclosure, and devotion to understanding and protecting the perplexing trap of life on The planet. To acquire further bits of knowledge into the difficulties, wins, and developing stories inside these domains, we leave on a progression of meetings with scholars and preservationists. Through these discussions, we plan to uncover the accounts that shape their work, dive into the intricacies of biological protection, and investigate the cooperative connection among science and promotion.

1. **Voices from the Field: The Scholar's Point of view**
   1. **The Call of Interest**
      In our most memorable meeting, Dr. Sarah Rodriguez, a carefully prepared field researcher, ponders the underlying flash that touched off her energy for science. "Interest is the main thrust," she underlines. "Whether it's the unobtrusive subtleties of creature conduct or the multifaceted designs of vegetation, science offers an endless excursion of investigation."
   2. **The Adventure of Disclosure**
      Dr. Rodriguez depicts the elation of finding new species. "Every endeavor is an expedition," she shares. "The second you coincidentally find an animal groups never reported, it's a mix of energy and a significant feeling of obligation to defend that biodiversity."
   3. **Protection Difficulties**

In any case, the researcher recognizes the difficulties in the field. "Living space misfortune, environmental change, and human effect present huge dangers. It's a test of skill and endurance to record and comprehend species before they disappear."

II. **Watchmen of Biodiversity: Preservationists in real life**

1. **The Development of Preservation**
   Our subsequent meeting highlights Imprint Thompson, a progressive devoted to protecting biodiversity. He talks about the development of preservation endeavors throughout the long

term. "It's not just about safeguarding species; it's tied in with safeguarding whole biological systems. Preservation has become more comprehensive, perceiving the interconnectedness of every living thing."

2. **Preservation as Promotion**
Thompson underlines the job of promotion in preservation. "We're not simply working with environments; we're working with networks. Preservation is tied in with building spans, encouraging comprehension, and engaging nearby populaces to become stewards of their regular legacy."

3. **Examples of overcoming adversity**

The protectionist shares examples of overcoming adversity, featuring projects that have exhibited the positive effect of devoted endeavors. "From the recuperation of imperiled species to the reclamation of debased territories, these examples of overcoming adversity fuel our assurance to proceed with the battle for biodiversity."

III. Crossing Accounts: Where Science Meets Protection

1. **Overcoming any issues**
Our third meeting highlights Dr. Emily Harper, whose work spans the universes of science and preservation. "There's many times a hole among examination and activity," she notes. "It is crucial for "Overcome that issue. What benefit is information on the off chance that it doesn't convert into substantial protection measures?"

2. **Cooperative Preservation**
Dr. Harper highlights the significance of joint effort. "Protection is a multidisciplinary exertion. It's not simply researchers; it's policymakers, local area pioneers, and general society. We want aggregate activity to address the perplexing difficulties our planet faces."

3. **Moral Contemplations**

The scholar and preservationist wrestles with moral contemplations in examination and protection. "As we endeavor to comprehend and safeguard biodiversity, moral contemplations are foremost. Offsetting logical request with the prosperity of biological systems and networks is a continuous test."

IV. The Eventual fate of Science and Protection: Looking Forward

1. **Mechanical Advancements**

   Our fourth interviewee, Dr. James Turner, digs into the job of innovation in forming the fate of science and protection. "Mechanical advancements, from DNA sequencing to satellite checking, are reforming our capacity to study and safeguard biodiversity. These instruments give extraordinary experiences and illuminate designated preservation procedures."

2. **Environmental Change Flexibility**

   Dr. Turner examines the major problem of environmental change. "Environmental change is modifying territories at a disturbing rate. Our future endeavors should zero in on alleviation as well as on improving the versatility of biological systems to adjust to these changes."

3. **Enabling the Future**

Every one of our interviewees express a common obligation to sustaining the up and coming age of scholars and preservationists. "Instruction is critical," they consistently concur. "Motivating another age of researchers and promoters is our best interest coming down the line for biodiversity."

8.2 Anecdotes and Stories from Fishermen and Local Communities

In the core of waterfront networks, where the rhythms of life are entwined with the back and forth movement of the ocean, anglers become narrators, and the sea turns into a limitless repository of stories.

This exposition sets out on an excursion to unwind the tales and stories that reverberation through the ages of anglers and nearby networks. From stories of powerful gets to experiences with slippery ocean animals, these accounts not just narrative the vocations of those ward on the ocean yet additionally weave a social embroidery mirroring the significant association among mankind and the sea world.

1. **The Angler's Legend: Stories of the Catch**
1. **The Special case that will always stand out**
   Each carefully prepared angler has a story of "the special case that will always stand out." Whether a goliath marlin or an unbelievable grouper, these accounts are carved in sea legend. Juan Rodriguez, an endured angler from a little beach front town, describes with a gleam in his expression, "I had it, No doubt. The greatest fish these waters at any point saw. However, it had different plans, got away like a shadow in the profound."
2. **Hitting the dance floor with the Sharks**

Sharks, the superb leaders of the sea, frequently highlight conspicuously in anglers' accounts. Miguel Hernandez, an angler with many years of involvement, shares a nerve racking experience, "There was this extraordinary white, a behemoth. It orbited our boat for a really long time, similar to a quiet dance. We felt the beat of the sea, the fragile harmony among hunter and prey."

II. **Secrets of the Profound: Folktales and Legends**

1. **The Mermaid's Regret**
   In seaside networks, mermaids are legendary animals as well as celebrated occupants of the profound. Maria Lopez, an angler's girl, recaps a story went down through ages, "My grandma swore she heard a mermaid singing on twilight evenings. An eerie tune that discussed love and misfortune, reverberating across the waves."
2. **The Phantom Boat**

Rumors from far and wide suggest that a phantom boat, embellished with worn out sails and directed by ghost mariners, wanders the untamed ocean. Antonio Ramirez, a senior in a waterfront town, shares an account of a far off experience, "On a hazy evening, we witnessed the phantom boat. A ghastly vessel cruising quietly, conveying stories of mariners lost adrift, perpetually exploring the limit between the living and the hereafter."

III. Practical Insight: Stories of Protection and Stewardship

1. **The Story of the Insightful Senior**
   In each fishing local area, there's a senior adored for shrewdness in maintainable practices. Rosa Martinez, a local area pioneer, shares the narrative of Wear Carlos, "He instructed us that the ocean is liberal yet requests regard. Wear Carlos could peruse the flows, the indications of the climate, passing down information that guaranteed we could look for ages without draining our seas."
2. **The Watchman Turtle**

A few stories rise above fables and become watchmen of preservation. Nearby people group frequently share stories of an insightful ocean turtle directing anglers to prolific grounds. As Miguel Hernandez describes, "When the old turtle surfaces, we follow. It resembles she knows where the overflow is, advising us that congruity with nature is the way in to a plentiful reap."

IV. Evolving Tides: Accounts of Transformation and Versatility

1. **The Tempest's Anger**
   Anglers' accounts likewise give testimony regarding the changing environment and the tempests that characterize seaside presence. Juan Rodriguez describes enduring a savage tempest, "The waves overshadowed us like monsters. It was a fight against the components, an indication of nature's unforgiving power. Yet, we adjust, reconstruct, and proceed."

2. **The Tough Soul**

In the midst of ecological difficulties, stories arise of networks tough despite difficulty. Maria Lopez shares, "Our town confronted a decrease in fish stocks, however we adjusted. Economical practices, local area drives — our accounts are presently about strength, about flourishing together as one with the ocean."

V. Passing the Light: Stories as Social Legacy

1. **The Fisherfolk Celebration**
   In beach front towns, yearly celebrations praise the rich embroidery of stories. These occasions become stages to pass down customs, as Rosa Martinez portrays, "The Fisherfolk Celebration is in excess of a festival; it's a living chronicle of our accounts. Youthful and old assemble to share encounters, guaranteeing our sea legacy perseveres."
2. **Stories by the Fire**

A night by the fire is a study hall where older folks share stories with the future. Antonio Ramirez stresses the significance, "Our accounts aren't simply diversion; they convey shrewdness. By the fire, the examples of the ocean are granted, guaranteeing that the tradition of our sea culture lives on."

8.3 Historical Accounts and Legends Surrounding Lesser-Known Fish

The oceanic domain, with its puzzling profundities and overflowing life, has been a wellspring of interest all through mankind's set of experiences. In this investigation, we set out on an excursion through chance to reveal verifiable records and legends encompassing less popular fish. From old developments to sea societies, these stories weave a story that rises above the logical, digging into the domains of fantasy, legends, and the persevering through secrets hid underneath the waves.

1. **Old Viewpoints: Fish in Folklore and Imagery**
1. **Mesopotamian Fish Divinities**
   In the support of civilization, the Tigris and Euphrates streams led to fantasies entwining fish with divine imagery. The Sumerians respected Enki, a god frequently portrayed with the lower body of a fish. Enki was the lord of shrewdness, freshwater, and creation, underlining the importance old societies ascribed to fish in figuring out the secrets of life.
2. **Fish in Egyptian Iconography**

Egyptian folklore additionally embraced the imagery of fish. The tilapia, a typical Nile fish, represented ripeness and overflow. Besides, the goddess Hatmehit was depicted as a fish, stressing the heavenly association with oceanic life.

II. **Sea Fables: Fish as Society Legends and Reprobates**

1. **The Unbelievable Coelacanth**
   The coelacanth, an ancient fish remembered to have become terminated with the dinosaurs, reemerged in the Comoros Islands in 1938, starting both logical interest and neighborhood old stories. Anglers in the district made stories of the coelacanth as a watchman soul, an animal exemplifying the versatility of the sea.
2. **The Baffling Oarfish**

The oarfish, with its long, snake like appearance, has caught the creative mind of sea societies. Japanese legends depicts the oarfish as the courier of the ocean god's royal residence, an extraordinary element predicting quakes and torrents. The oarfish in this manner turns into an animal riding the domains of the real world and legend.

III. **Archaic Wonders: Oceanic Monsters and Irregularities**

1. **The Ocean Priest and Ocean Minister**
   Middle age European records are packed with depictions of

secretive ocean animals, frequently deciphered from a perspective of strict or legendary convictions. The ocean priest and ocean diocesan, for instance, were portrayed as sea-going clerical figures, encapsulating the obscure miracles hiding underneath the waves.

2. **The Supposed Ocean Snake Sightings**

Middle age mariners' diaries once in a while recorded sightings of ocean snakes, lengthened animals with snake like elements. These records, while frequently adorned, mirror the interest and fear that less popular marine species enlivened in nautical networks.

IV. Nautical Notions: Fish as Harbingers of Fortune or Adversity

1. **The Fortunate Flying Fish**
   In oceanic legend, flying fish are viewed as images of best of luck. Mariners accepted that the presence of flying fish showed fair climate and a plentiful catch. This notion mirrors the cozy association between nautical networks and the animals possessing the waters they explored.
2. **The Evil Sign of the Herring Gull**

On the other hand, the herring gull was respected with doubt by mariners. Its presence was viewed as an evil sign, flagging the possible beginning of tempests. Nautical notions, for example, these highlight the well established convictions encompassing less popular fish in sea societies.

V. Investigation and Disclosure: Experiences with the New

1. **The Bewildering Mola**
   The sea sunfish, or mola, with its unconventional appearance and tremendous size, confounded early wayfarers. Accounts from mariners experiencing this monstrous fish depict it as a strange animal, frequently confused because of its particular shape and propensity for lolling close to the water's surface.

2. The Puzzling Gulper Eel

The gulper eel, with its enormous mouth and bioluminescent bait, is one more illustration of a less popular fish that mixed interest and hypothesis. Early submarine investigations uncovered this remote ocean occupant, testing assumptions and powering the interest with the secrets concealed in the sea's profundities.

VI. Contemporary Points of view: Adjusting Science and Legend

1. The Revelation of the Coelacanth: Logical Wonder or Legend Affirmed?
   The rediscovery of the coelacanth in the twentieth century fills in as an extension between logical request and old stories. Once consigned to fantasy, the coelacanth arose as a living fossil, a demonstration of the strength of specific species against the tide of time.
2. The Job of Preservation in Molding Stories

Contemporary stories encompassing less popular fish progressively interlace with protection endeavors. As mindfulness develops with respect to jeopardized species, accounts shift from legendary animals to dire calls for insurance. The situation of species like the vaquita or the Fiends Opening pupfish turns into a cutting edge story, convincing social orders to change their relationship with these animals.

VII. Social Importance: Fish in Craftsmanship, Writing, and Cooking

1. Fish as Creative Images
   All through craftsmanship and writing, fish have filled in as strong images. From antiquated cave artworks to Renaissance works of art, piscine themes frequently convey more profound implications connected with otherworldliness, change, and the ephemerality of life.

2. Culinary Stories: From the Banquet to the Imperiled Dish

In culinary domains, certain fish species change from being simple fixings to social images. Stories of excessive fish feasts in authentic dinners balance forcefully with accounts of jeopardized luxuries, mirroring the developing connection between human social orders and the amphibian world.

VIII. The Fate of Fish Stories: Protection, Investigation, and Social Safeguarding

1. **The Moral Component of Accounts**
   In contemporary talk, the account encompassing less popular fish is progressively mixed with moral contemplations. Protection stories underscore the significance of mindful fishing rehearses, environment safeguarding, and the relief of human effects on marine biological systems.
2. **Adjusting Logical Investigation and Social Safeguarding**

As mechanical progressions take into consideration more profound investigation of the sea's secrets, there is a sensitive equilibrium to strike between logical request and social protection. Guaranteeing that native information and customary stories are regarded and safeguarded becomes necessary to a comprehensive comprehension of less popular fish.

www.ingramcontent.com/pod-product-compliance
Lightning Source LLC
Chambersburg PA
CBHW071951201224
19274CB00045B/499